Praise for *The Ambition Trap*

"*The Ambition Trap* is a paradigm-shifter for anyone who's ever felt caught between desire and self-doubt. With compassion and clarity, this book reframes ambition . . . as an inherent right everyone is entitled to claim. . . . It reveals how ambition, when grounded in authenticity, can ignite powerful cultural transformations. *The Ambition Trap* goes beyond granting permission to dream big—it boldly encourages us to embrace our gifts with confidence and unapologetic determination."
—Gay Hendricks, bestselling author of *Five Wishes* and *The Big Leap*

"In Amina AlTai's glorious new book, she allows us to reframe our relationship to ambition, particularly the vilification of it, to embrace a more positive version. . . . For everyone looking to understand themselves and underlying societal systems that hold perceptions of ambition in place, AlTai offers insight and actionable ideas for a new definition of your ambition and yourself."
—Stacy London, stylist, designer, midlife advocate, and *New York Times* bestselling author

"AlTai's book is a beautiful offering for those looking to explore their fullest potential and to do so with wholeness and integrity. She shows us that these pieces are not mutually exclusive but essential components of how we can thrive by aligning our ambitions with our desire to positively impact the world and be transformed in the process. It is a kind and clear call to action for those looking to step into their greatest potential."
—Matt McGorry, actor, activist, and empowerment coach

"Smart, nuanced, and inclusive, AlTai takes a taboo topic and makes it feel accessible to everyone. With warmth and clarity, she encourages us to stop chasing external validation and instead align our ambitions with who we truly are."
—Sahaj Kaur Kohli, author of *But What Will People Say?*

"Amina AlTai challenges the notion that ambition has to mean sacrificing our well-being. This book is for anyone tired of the hustle and ready to create meaningful work and a life they truly love."   —Minda Harts, bestselling author of *The Memo*

"*The Ambition Trap* is a transformative guide for anyone feeling overwhelmed by the pressure to succeed and seeking a more sustainable and authentic relationship with ambition."
—Lauren McGoodwin, founder of Career Contessa and author of *Power Moves*

"In *The Ambition Trap*, Amina AlTai redefines what it means to succeed in a world dominated by hustle culture. . . . For anyone ready to step off the treadmill and live a life of true achievement and joy, *The Ambition Trap* is the inspiring roadmap you've been waiting for."   —Claire Wasserman, founder and author of *Ladies Get Paid*

"*The Ambition Trap* is a refreshing read for anyone who's ever felt stuck between wanting more and doubting themself. With a warm, down-to-earth approach, this book flips the script on ambition—it's not something to hold back but a right everyone should embrace . . . it dares you to go all-in on your wildest desires."
—Jamila Souffrant—author of *Your Journey to Financial Freedom*, and host of *Journey to Launch* podcast

THE AMBITION TRAP

THE
AMBITION
TRAP

HOW TO STOP CHASING
AND START LIVING

———◇———

Amina AlTai

THE OPEN FIELD / PENGUIN LIFE

VIKING
An imprint of Penguin Random House LLC
1745 Broadway, New York, NY 10019
penguinrandomhouse.com

The Open Field/A Penguin Life Book

THE OPEN FIELD is a registered trademark of MOS Enterprises, Inc.

VIKING is a registered trademark of Penguin Random House LLC.

Line art by Samantha Sedlack

Designed by Amanda Dewey

LIBRARY OF CONGRESS CATALOGING-IN-PUBLICATION DATA
Names: AlTai, Amina, author.
Title: The ambition trap: how to get what you really
want when getting ahead hurts / Amina AlTai.
Description: [New York] : The Open Field/Penguin Life, [2025] |
Includes bibliographical references and index.
Identifiers: LCCN 2024043597 (print) | LCCN 2024043598 (ebook) |
ISBN 9780593655306 (hardcover) | ISBN 9780593655313 (ebook)
Subjects: LCSH: Burn out (Psychology) | Goal (Psychology) | Ambition.
Classification: LCC BF481 .A48 2025 (print) |
LCC BF481 (ebook) | DDC 158.7—dc23/eng/20250129
LC record available at https://lccn.loc.gov/2024043597
LC ebook record available at https://lccn.loc.gov/2024043598

Printed in the United States of America
1st Printing

The authorized representative in the EU for product safety and
compliance is Penguin Random House Ireland, Morrison Chambers,
32 Nassau Street, Dublin D02 YH68, Ireland,
https://eu-contact.penguin.ie.

MARIA SHRIVER

PRESENTS

THE OPEN FIELD

A PUBLISHING IMPRINT

BOOKS THAT RISE ABOVE THE NOISE AND MOVE HUMANITY FORWARD

Dear Reader,

Years ago, these words attributed to Rumi found a place in my heart:

> *Out beyond ideas of*
> *wrongdoing and rightdoing,*
> *there is a field. I'll meet you there.*

Ever since, I've cultivated an image of what I call "the Open Field"—a place out beyond fear and shame, beyond judgment, loneliness, and expectation. A place that hosts the reunion of all creation. It's the hope of my soul to find my way there—and whenever I hear an insight or a practice that helps me on the path, I love nothing more than to share it with others.

That's why I've created The Open Field. My hope is to publish books that honor the most unifying truth in human life: We are all seeking the same things. We're all seeking dignity. We're all seeking joy. We're all seeking love and acceptance, seeking to be seen, to be safe. And there is no competition for these things we seek—because they are not material goods; they are spiritual gifts!

We can all give each other these gifts if we share what we know—what has lifted us up and moved us forward. That is our duty to one another—to help each other toward acceptance, toward peace, toward happiness—and my promise to you is that the books published under this imprint will be maps to the Open Field, written by guides who know the path and want to share it.

Each title will offer insights, inspiration, and guidance for moving beyond the fears, the judgments, and the masks we all wear. And when we take off the masks, guess what? We will see that we are the opposite of what we thought—we are each other.

We are all on our way to the Open Field. We are all helping one another along the path. I'll meet you there.

Love, Maria S

This book is dedicated to anyone who has lived at the margins, who knows the unspeakable pain of being told we are too something—too weird, too dark, too queer, too foreign, too big, too poor, too feminine, or too disabled—to sit at the table. For the ones who have been told we are not enough because we don't conform to the narrow confines of what this world calls typical. For the ones who've spent their lives trying to change themselves when, all along, it was the system that needed changing. Let this book be your reminder: Everything is right with us. And it would be the deepest honor if you would sit with me, just as you are.

I want to unfold. Let no place in me hold itself closed,

for where I am closed, I am false.

—Rainer Maria Rilke,
Book of Hours: Love Poems to God[1]

CONTENTS

———◇———

Part I
WHY YOUR RELATIONSHIP TO AMBITION ISN'T WORKING

Part II
EMBODYING PURPOSEFUL AMBITION

AUTHOR'S NOTE

I want to address a few things before we begin. First, it is of the utmost importance to revere and respect the lineage from which knowledge emerges. I honor and pay homage to the teachers and teachings that have informed and inspired my work. My teachers, coaches, mentors, and influences include Rha Goddess, JLove Calderón, Hildie Dunn, Erin Foley, Jesse Johnson Chandra, Sri Kala Chandra, Handel Group, Institute of Integrative Nutrition, Dr. Deganit Nuur, Anurag Gupta, Heather Box, Dr. Margarita Russolello, Shamanic Reiki Worldwide, Eileen Lawlor, Amy Bonaduce-Gardner, Charlie Knoles, Rachel Rodgers, and Ben Turshen.

On General Terminologies

Throughout the book I reference historically excluded and underrecognized leaders, marginalized groups, BIPOC, and white supremacy culture. To support our shared understanding, I've defined those terms herein.

The vocabulary I use around any data points refers to the language I encountered during my data collection that was used by my sources. There may be instances where I use gender binary language, as that is the language in which the data appeared. Language and vocabulary are shifting quickly, and I try to always take cues from communities that are driving the change. However, I am still using whatever language appeared in data collection to make sure the data reflects its original intentions and is therefore clear to the reader. It does not always reflect my preferences in how to address my communities.

Historically excluded: When I refer to historically excluded people, I refer to those who have been denied access to equal opportunities or suffered institutional discrimination. This definition includes women, birthing parents, women of color, BIPOC, those with disabilities both visible and invisible, the chronically ill, neurodivergent people, those of varied body shapes and sizes, and the LGBTQIA+ community.[1] Though none of these groups are monoliths, and each experiences varying levels of discrimination, we know they face more challenges than cisgender heterosexual white men. I may also refer to these historically excluded people as "underrecognized leaders."

Marginalized: Marginalized people are those who experience discrimination and exclusion due to imbalanced power dynamics. Marginalization can occur across races, genders, ethnicities, abilities, ages, body shapes or sizes, religions, documentation statuses, and sexual orientations. By definition, diverse, BIPOC, and historically excluded leaders are often marginalized.[2]

BIPOC: The term "BIPOC" means Black, Indigenous, and people of color. You may see a variation of this in the text such as "QTBIPOC," which stands for queer, trans, Black, Indigenous, and people of color. This term is currently being debated within those communities. Although the term exists to express unity and solidarity, the groups it represents could not be more different. Additionally, some scholars argue that the more we introduce new labels in reference to non-white groups, the more we actually center whiteness in America. I made this style choice because it's a readily understood term.

White supremacy culture: White supremacy culture is defined as a form of racism that perpetuates the idea that white people are superior to people of other races and therefore should dominate them economically, politically, and socially.[3] Attributes of white supremacy appear within organizational culture and are accepted as norms and standards without deliberate acknowledgment or consensus from the entire group. These attributes have a detrimental impact on both individuals of color and white individuals because they prioritize the values, preferences, and experiences of a single racial group over all others. Even organizations led by individuals of color or predominantly composed of people of color can exhibit these characteristics associated with white supremacy culture. It's important to note that we are all navigating this culture, regardless of our racial identity or intersectionality—however, we are not all affected in the same ways. There can be a tendency to hear the phrase "white supremacy culture" as a personal attack on white people. It is not. It is a culture we are all harmed by. A simple example of this is living in a culture that teaches us to disconnect from our physical selves and prioritize thinking above feeling, and therefore not acknowledge the valuable wisdom our bodies provide.

On Case Studies

Finally, to preserve the anonymity of my clients, the case studies used in this book are a mix of actual and fictitious events. In some cases, it felt important to preserve the real aspects of people's stories to bring the work to life in a more tangible way. In these instances, we asked permission to include their stories. To protect the privacy of certain individuals, their names and identifying details have been changed.

FOREWORD

by Rachel Rodgers

I can't work today" was all I could say.

I had called my assistant in tears. I didn't know what was happening but my heart was racing, my thoughts weren't clear, I felt physically ill, and I knew I finally had to stop.

Stopping was my greatest fear.

I had been on a tear the past couple of months. (But really? All my life.) Trying to do it all and giving myself zero grace. I refused to fail at anything no matter how many chips were stacked against me. I was going to be the perfect wife, mother, and professional. Not a single ball would drop on my watch.

Until I dropped every single ball. They came crashing down in dramatic, spectacular fashion. I was in the middle of a major case at work and I could not function as a professional. I had a brand-new baby at home and I couldn't do anything for my child except sit on the couch with him, breastfeed, and snuggle. I had nothing to offer my husband, who had to do everything for our household while my baby and I perpetually lay on the couch. I barely had the strength or desire to eat. Let alone talk or do anything else.

What I am describing here is my experience with burnout. It's very real, very scary, and very common for ambitious professionals of historically excluded backgrounds. Despite the many systems of oppression working against us, we insist on outworking those systems. We refuse to be held back. So we work. And we work. And we work some more. Until we fall flat on our faces. Or sadly, in some cases, until we die.

If you picked up this book in a similar moment of existential crisis, burnout, or being plain pissed off about the state of work, you're about to learn how to break free.

I've had the privilege of knowing Amina as a friend, colleague, and client, and let me tell you, this woman brings fire and insight like no one else. She is all about grace, boundary setting, and vision—making her a thought leader whose words are like a balm to the recovering workaholic's soul.

So let's get real about ambition. For those of us who are women, BIPOC, LGBTQIA+, immigrants, and other folks who don't fit in the whitewashed frame of success, we've heard mixed messages our whole lives. Be ambitious, but not too ambitious. Speak up, but not too loud. Hustle hard, but be "likable." It's a trap. This contradictory messaging creates a constant push and pull, making ambition feel dangerous or even illicit—something only acceptable when it neatly fits within the narrow boundaries set by someone else's standards.

This, of course, makes it harder for us to own our ambitions. We start to question whether what we want is valid, whether we're asking for too much, or whether we're even deserving of the things we desire. The lie society feeds us is insidious: ambition, for some of us, is an audacious overreach—a privilege only afforded to those who have already been granted a seat at the table. This lie tells us that the mere act of wanting more makes us ungrateful, greedy, or unworthy. But none of this is true.

That's why Amina's work is so damn powerful. *The Ambition Trap* is more than just a book—it's a reclamation of ambition for those of us who've been told we have no right to it. Amina deftly dives into how ambition, when nurtured from a place of wholeness rather than pain or scarcity, can be transformed into a dynamic force that propels us toward creating real, lasting change. This book doesn't just validate our desires; it empowers us to fully own them, unapologetically.

Because that's what we deserve.

I know firsthand, as a business coach and advocate for equity and representation, how powerful ambition can be when it's freed from the oppressive constraints of societal expectations. I see the magic that happens when underrecognized people step out of the shadows and claim their space, demanding that the world see them not just as survivors but as visionaries, innovators, and change-makers. But I also see the weight of the barriers they have to overcome, the persistent messages of insufficiency that tell them to shrink rather than expand.

The framework outlined in this book will take you on a journey that'll change the way you do business, build your career, and live your life. Amina will compassionately guide you away from seeking validation outside yourself and inward, so you can confidently build the life you truly want. And yes, it's permission to be unapologetically ambitious—because let's be clear, ambition is natural and neutral. It's our divine right. And when you align that ambition with purpose, magic happens.

THE PERMISSION YOU DIDN'T KNOW YOU NEEDED

Simply put: This book is a permission slip to chase your wildest dreams (the key word being "your"). Not the dreams sold to you by society. With practical exercises and stories that will have you nodding along, Amina helps you explore your unique gifts, values, and the impact you want to make on the world. She's offering all of us a lifeline—a way to step out of the bullshit trap of balancing "too much" and "not enough"—and to finally live your ambition out loud.

I wish I had had this book years ago when I was lying on the couch, burnt out and lost.

Amina, thank you for this work, for your vulnerability, and for sharing your story so openly. This book is a gift to anyone who's ever felt torn between chasing more and settling for less. My advice to you, dear reader? Dive in, soak up every word, and let this book show you how to be fiercely, joyfully ambitious on your own terms.

xo,

RACHEL RODGERS

INTRODUCTION

It was a sweltering summer Friday in Manhattan. By eight a.m., the streets were already filled with people in a state of agitation over another heat advisory. The air was sticky with humidity, forcing my dress against my legs like a damp cloth. I hopped into a little red MINI Cooper, the Zipcar I had rented for the day, the steering wheel almost too hot to touch. I safely placed my work tote and laptop onto the passenger seat as if it were a companion. Then I blasted the AC, pulled out of the parking garage, and floored it.

I flew up I-95, making my way from New York City to Connecticut to visit a client for our regular Friday meeting. Like many career-driven perfectionists, I loathed being late. I wove in and out of traffic, jerking the car across lanes to avoid slowdowns. I had already clocked a sixty-hour workweek and was eager to get to the weekend.

And then my phone rang.

I quickly glanced at the caller ID on what would now be a vintage iPhone and saw it was my physician, Dr. Gulati, who was calling.

"Hello!" I answered, rather annoyed. I didn't need anything slowing me down.

"Where are you?" Dr. Gulati asked, sounding panicked. There was a strain in her voice and an urgency in her tone that I'd never heard from her before.

"Driving to my client . . . can we make this quick?" I said, a bit dismissively.

I could hear her sipping the air in on the other end of the phone, taking a deep breath, and I was curious what she was steadying herself for. I will never forget what she said next.

"If you don't go to the hospital now, instead of going to your client, you will be days away from multiple organ failure."

I blinked hard, not quite comprehending what she was saying.

"Wait, what do you mean?"

"You have become dangerously anemic," Dr. Gulati said. "Without IV infusions, you are at risk of widespread organ dysfunction and possibly failure."

The last few years flashed before my eyes. Building a company, achieving major milestones, the good-girl tendencies. *How could this have happened to me?* I asked myself. *I did everything "right."*

I didn't know it then, but I had inadvertently fallen into what I later would call "the ambition trap."

It turned out I had celiac disease and Hashimoto's thyroiditis, and because I was not taking care of myself, I had lost the ability to absorb critical minerals. Because I was too ill to take a gradual approach, in the weeks to come I had to work with a hematologist to use intravenous therapies to restore my health. But the diagnoses (and my genetics) weren't the real problem; me and my mind were. My workaholic tendencies and painful relationship to success were—quite literally—killing me.

THE WAY WE'RE WORKING ISN'T WORKING

In the decade-plus since my near-death experience, I have told this story on countless stages and podcasts. The one thing that is never lost on me is how many people queue up or message me after to tell me they have a very similar story—and it wouldn't surprise me if you had one, too. How could that be? How could so many of us be working ourselves into pain and suffering?

After my health scare, I started to put my ambition under the microscope and a distressing though very common pattern emerged. Probably like many of you reading this, I started my career just before one of the worst economic declines in US history. Late-stage capitalism taught me to derive my value, self-worth, and identity from perpetually competing through jobs and by gathering achievements. I learned to put my head down, work hard, and hustle tirelessly. Like many of us ambitious folks coming of age at this time, I felt like my work wasn't just a job but my whole personality. This ethos no doubt cost me my relationships, my hobbies, and ultimately my physical and mental health.

Can you relate? Maybe you've also tried to outwork (whether consciously or unconsciously) everyone in the room to prove your value, and it's made you sick.

Maybe you've been chasing achievements, money, and titles, but it now feels empty and pointless.

Maybe you're battling your way to the top but feel crushed by the microaggressions and are wondering if it's worth it.

Maybe you're having an existential crisis of your own, as the peak of the mountain you just climbed doesn't feel like the dream you had in mind at all.

One of the challenges in the way we've come to be in relationship with ambition is that we believe it has a never-ending upward trajectory—that being ambitious means never stopping, never taking a break. In fact, the pervasive impression of all-things-ambitious is about more growth at all times, no matter the cost. This has caused many of us to reject ambition altogether, to see it as a dirty word. But let's make one thing clear—ambition is neutral and natural.

WHAT WE THINK AMBITION IS

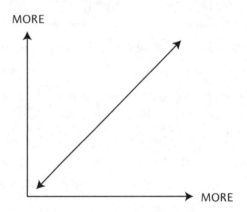

I am, by no means, asking you to be less successful or to renounce your ambition. In fact, I am one of the most ambitious people I know, and I bet you are, too. What I am inviting you to do is to be in the right relationship with it.

The reality is, ambition in its purest form isn't about more for more's sake no matter the cost. It's about cultivation, pacing, replenishing, nurturing, resting, and growth. Our ambition goes in cycles, just as a perennial flower's growth does. It starts with a seedling of desire: *I want to grow*. We nurture and water that desire by nurturing ourselves. We pace our growth, and inch by inch we rise. We become as tall as we can in each moment, based on our inner and outer states. Our gifts come into full bloom, and we have a seasonal peak. It's glorious. And then the winds shift, and we feel we can grow no more. So we pause, slow down, and go back underground to prepare ourselves for another season. The cycle repeats over and over again.

WHAT AMBITION ACTUALLY IS

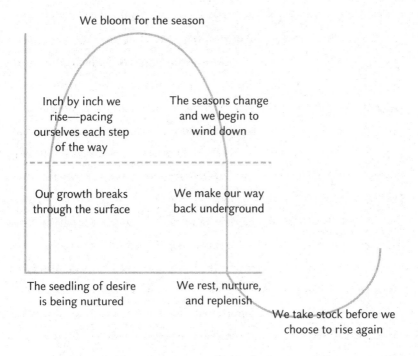

We bloom for the season

Inch by inch we rise—pacing ourselves each step of the way

The seasons change and we begin to wind down

Our growth breaks through the surface

We make our way back underground

The seedling of desire is being nurtured

We rest, nurture, and replenish

We take stock before we choose to rise again

But there are a few ways ambition gets distorted. First, "ambition" is one of those culturally complex, politically loaded words that manages to highlight either our defects or our strengths, depending on who is being labeled. Ambitious women are often considered "too much," for example, while ambitious men are seen as driven and powerful.[1]

This also affects how we get to be ambitious. Women are told to speak up, but when we speak truth to power, we are told our experiences aren't real. People of color are told to take up space in organizations, but when we share the truth of our experiences, we are told it's inconvenient. Those of us with disabilities are told to place our hats in the ring, but our needs and basic accommodations are bypassed, leading us to underperform or overperform in ways that further exacerbate our illness, injury, or disability. We are often told *to be* and *not to be* in the very same sentence.

I often think of Serena Williams's 2018 US Open Women's Singles final. She was playing the up-and-comer Naomi Osaka, and the game took a turn. Issues began in this now infamous match when Serena's coach, Patrick Mouratoglou, made a hand gesture toward her in the second set. The umpire gave her a penalty for cheating, ruling that the gesture was actually coaching. When she fought back, she received two more game penalties, eventually losing the match.

For much of her career, Williams has been relentlessly dinged for her ambition, authenticity, race, and gender. In her own words, "I don't cheat to win. I'd rather lose."[2] Coming to her defense, tennis legend Billie Jean King said, "When a woman is emotional, she's 'hysterical' and she's penalized for it. When a man does the same, he's 'outspoken' and there are no repercussions. Thank you, Serena Williams, for calling out this double standard."[3] The umpire, his beliefs undoubtedly shaped by the patriarchy, questioned her right to claim her space at the top and stacked the deck against her. And it's not that different for the people I coach.

Perhaps you've had your own experience of this.

Maybe you were finally named CEO but the experience has been rife with headwinds and you've never felt more exhausted or empty in your life.

Perhaps you rose to the heights of a career in academia only to be taken down for the very perspectives you were originally valued for.

Maybe you even started your own business because that is what you thought you should do but getting your slice of the 2.4 percent of VC funding[4] has been a total nightmare and it feels impossible to keep going.

Ambition is complicated—especially for historically excluded people.

IDENTITY AND AMBITION

For many underrecognized people, the crux of this challenging relationship with ambition lies in the way our identity intersects with certain cultural beliefs about who can and can't be ambitious. If you're a woman, a person of color, a queer or disabled person, or part of any other marginalized demographic, due to the various isms—racism, sexism, classism, homophobia, transphobia, sizeism, xenophobia, and all the other prejudices that tell us we're not enough—advancing is often not without major double binds. In the attempt to be ambitious, we are confronted by irreconcilable demands and choices that impact our minds, bodies, and paths forward. We come to believe that through working harder, being smarter, or being "perfect," we can prove to the world that we are "enough." But the world is often too quick to respond back that enoughness is only possible for a certain group of people. We are taught that power and success looks *one way*: white, straight, able-bodied, and male. (It's important to underscore that cisgender white men are not a monolith. For every problematic white male leader I've encountered, I've also met ones who are committed to allyship.) The truth is, the world has been designed by them and for them. Perpetually placing them in positions of power creates a lot of the systemic barriers we experience today.

Therefore, to get where we want to go, many of us end up contorting into the more socially acceptable versions of ourselves. We spend our lifetimes code-switching so those in power feel comfortable in our presence; in fact, we are taught that our value is correlated to the comfort they feel around us. And all of this shape-shifting weighs heavy on us until we collapse emotionally, physically, and spiritually under the massiveness of it all. If we're not careful, these behaviors become a generational cycle. We encounter these dynamics so frequently because few of us are encouraged to value our real selves and our unique contributions in the workplace.

I know more about these dynamics than I would care to admit. As a third-culture kid (I'm half-Iraqi, half-Welsh, and grew up in the US) who was raised Muslim and entered the workforce during the very racialized, Islamophobic years immediately following 9/11, where it didn't feel safe to be in my brownness, to say that my relationship with success, taking up space, and being seen was distorted would be an understatement. But to really show you its roots, I need to tell you more about the family I grew up in.

THE ROOTS OF OUR AMBITION

Like a lot of us, I was raised in a challenging family system that was rife with physical and mental illness. My dad, Mohammed, has thick, black wavy hair and an even thicker accent. He was born and raised in Baghdad during much turmoil and government transition. Our family was intensely outspoken against the newly forming government's tyrannical forces—so much so that they, including my dad, were imprisoned and tortured. Though he speaks very little of this time, I know how deep his scars run.

In 1980, in the middle of his medical residency, my dad fled to the UK, where he later met my mother. Grappling with survivor's guilt, PTSD, and other mental health disorders made raising a family difficult. After a challenging start in the very hierarchical UK medical system, he was convinced that everything in America would be better. We became one of many families of immigrants running toward the American Dream.

It was the early '90s and the US was at war with Iraq, which I'm sure impacted my dad and his ambition more than I'll ever know. Growing up, we moved extensively as he tried desperately to find his place in the work world. As someone who had finished their medical training overseas, had deep brown skin, and had a name TSA flagged for decades, my dad found work to be filled with obstacles. He felt tremendous pressure as a survivor to do something big with his life and so was on a never-ending quest to become a famous surgeon, even when nothing seemed to work out. It was his painful relationship to ambition and his insatiable desire to be the smartest person in the room (where people often discounted him on identity alone) that invited me to deeply study my own relationship with work and worthiness.

Growing up, many of us likely watched family members have a distorted relationship with work and ambition, and those dynamics trickle down to influence us today. Maybe your immigrant mom had to overwork to make ends meet, and now you've maintained that same pace despite your current financial security. Or you saw the men in your family derive their power from their economic status, so now you do, too. What was modeled to us in childhood has ripple effects that can influence what we deem "typical," "acceptable," even "good" when it comes to ambition today.

Our core wounds, or earliest experiences of hurt and rejection, also distort our relationship with ambition. When my family first moved to the US, life seemed idyllic. I remember riding my tricycle back and forth across the concrete slab outside of our apartment building, eating vanilla ice cream on scorching summer afternoons, and playing on the swings with my older sister, Zahra. If this period in my family's life wasn't blissful, I didn't know it. A few years later, everything shifted. Zahra, who was eight at the time, was diagnosed with type 1 diabetes, and her devastating diagnosis rocked our family. Sensing the instability at home, I unconsciously decided not to add any additional burden to it. So I started to take on the role of the "glass child," which is the term used to describe siblings of a person with chronic illness or a disability.

Glass children are often overlooked and experience pressure to be problem-free and perfect so as not to add weight to the family system. When I was no longer able to get the attention and support I needed from my parents, I decided to be as self-sufficient and helpful as possible. We didn't have the term for it then, but I'm not sure it would have made a difference: I was the perfect glass child in all ways. These early experiences molded me into a hyper-independent perfectionist striving to be seen in a world that often prejudged me solely on my Arabic name and "exotic" looks.

Are you starting to see how I was set up for a wobbly relationship to ambition, all the way from childhood? Maybe you also have a story that mirrors this one. It turns out I'd been chasing my ambition from a place of pain and living according to others' definitions of success. The same is true for most of us. All of us have psychological wounds resulting from varying degrees of hurt, challenges, and trauma that have shaped our lives, and therefore our relationship to ambition, in different ways. Perhaps your parents were absent when you were growing up, so you're desperate to be seen and won't feel whole until you land that spot on TV. Maybe you were the academic underdog and want to prove your worth via several advanced degrees. Or maybe, like me, you had family members with chronic physical and mental illnesses and had to be so self-reliant that you felt nearly invisible, and thus built your whole life around your achievements so that you could feel seen. We all have a story, and unless we reconcile the pain in that story, it can direct our lives to unhealthy places.

But here's the rub. Even though my dad's tenuous relationship to striving, my being a glass child, and countless cultural forces shaped my relationship to ambition, I was the one hurting from the way I was living—so it was up to me to do something about it.

WHY I'M WRITING THIS BOOK

After my health crisis, I transitioned out of the business I had spent years building—a marketing agency—and instead took on a full-time role in the burgeoning wellness industry. While there, I enrolled in a coaching program with the hopes of turning my life around. This exploration felt great, and I wanted more. I pursued various certifications, studying nutrition, mindfulness, movement, and coaching. In Vedic philosophy, which I studied in my meditation training, they say, *Go toward what charms you.* I take that to mean, *Go toward the pull of your inner guidance.* Exploring all those subjects was my way of honoring my intuition. I wasn't entirely clear what I was going to do with these studies, but there was a sixth sense directing me toward them.

Though my roles in wellness marketing ended up being much healthier for me than the business I had built, I still sensed a profound disconnect from what I was doing and who I really was. I got the distinguished titles I wanted, yes, but I felt like I was playing a role on a stage not designed for me—and maybe that's how you're feeling right now. At the time, I remember thinking, *What the heck . . . this is the thing I thought I wanted? Why does it feel so terrible?* There was a part of me that was still chasing my ambition from a place of pain and doing the work I thought I s*hould* do.

After leaving another ill-fitting role in wellness marketing, I did what I always do: I dragged myself tearfully to my meditation cushion and sat there for weeks praying for a miracle. I have always been a spiritual person. I grew up in a religious home, where we were often encouraged to turn to God or a higher power for answers. To this day, when the truth doesn't feel readily apparent, I turn to my ancestors and guides for wisdom. This particular moment felt like an existential crisis—and something tells me you know this pain as well.

Then one day, while in deep meditation, my grandfather—or "jidu" as we say in Arabic—came to me and said, *Teach from you.* It wasn't unusual for my family elders to send me messages. Coming from two collectivist cultures, my grandparents were a huge part of my life. They were safety to me. They gave my family a place to stay when we were between homes, helped my parents pay the bills when they came up short, and were a source of unconditional love to me and my sisters. I always felt that both my earthside grandparents and my heavenly ones were looking out for me.

This time, however, I was a little freaked out by the message and questioned its validity. *Was that really my grandpa? Did I make this up because I'm so desperate for an answer?* But when I shared it with one of my teachers, Rha Goddess, she nodded along as if her ancestors visited her every day with such messages.

My jidu's words felt like an invitation to find more of myself and go deeper, and I decided to take his message to heart. After all, my career felt so wonky. I could no longer keep living as this wounded, compartmentalized version of myself chasing success in the way society defined it for me. It kept breaking my body and spirit. It even kept breaking my career. What harm could this do?

So I finally sat down to design my work and my life in a way that honored me in totality; not just my motivation and desires, but my need for rest and recovery as well. I combined my business background with my wellness tools, mindset training, energy healing, and coaching experience to design a curriculum that took a mind, body, soul—and career!—approach to living my purpose. I realized that when we bring all these pieces together, we can really, truly, actually *thrive*.

Following the process I created, I began to:

- Look at my mindset around achievement
- Examine my relationship to well-being, noticing where and why I was wringing every last drop of productivity out of my body and to what end

- Explore my core wounds and corresponding masks and the pain they were creating in my life

- Educate myself on the systems of oppression that hold historically excluded people back

- Have a very honest conversation with myself (and my guides) about what I'm called to do in this lifetime and how to do it

Along the way, I unearthed a compassionate route to my dreams, which I have now taught to thousands of clients—and which I am outlining for you in this book.

In part I, we will examine the forces driving our painful relationship to ambition—from our personal wounds and mindsets to the societal structures that shape our experiences—and the toll they take on us. Then in part II, we will learn how to design a life centered around purpose-fueled ambition, or the kind of growth that honors your greatest truth. We'll clarify your deepest calling, recognize and honor your innate gifts, and discover how to build a life grounded in contentment. My hope is that by the end of this book, you will feel empowered to pursue all of your desires in a way that nurtures you, your community, and the planet.

THERE'S NO BETTER TIME TO BREAK FREE FROM THE AMBITION TRAP

Unlike most popular self-help rhetoric, I believe the way to a healthier relationship with ambition isn't simply for us to work harder or only do the work at the individual level—hustle culture, the girl-boss era, and the pandemic years have underscored how broken this idea is. True success won't come from doing more but from being more ourselves, creating more ease, and doing this work as a *collective*. For real change to take place, the work on ourselves and the work on the collective must be equal.

Over the years as I grew my business, I became the go-to coach for historically excluded people, building a roster filled with notable female leaders, people of color, and queer and disabled visionaries. And I loved my job. I got a front-row seat to watching all these amazing leaders who had been long overlooked get their flowers. It gave me hope and served as evidence that change is possible. Few things have felt as gratifying.

Then 2020 happened. Just before the pandemic hit I had been feverishly traveling around the country giving talks, heading up trainings, and coaching leaders—and suddenly it all came to a grinding halt.

And then came May 25, 2020: the day George Floyd was murdered. His violent killing followed that of Breonna Taylor's in March and Ahmaud Arbery's in February of that same year, sparking demonstrations and uprisings around the globe. At the same time, I had been watching the staggering COVID-19 death rates of Black Americans with some horror. My Black clients didn't have to point it out; it was all over the news. Floyd's, Taylor's, and Arbery's murders, coupled with the staggering pandemic mortality rates of Black Americans, reinforced what many of us had long known to be true: Black lives are still treated as expendable in America. Once again, we were seeing that America's racial hierarchy was alive and well.

This racial hierarchy was also being reinforced through the world of work. That summer, we saw several prominent female business leaders being called into question for their inequitable business practices and racial biases. Among them was Reformation

CEO and founder Yael Aflalo on allegations of racism,[5] Man Repeller founder Leandra Medine Cohen for her "performative attempt to cover racist actions,"[6] and millennial luggage brand Away's co-founder and co-CEO Steph Korey for how she "regularly berated employees"[7] and "value[d] her own reputation over the well-being of the company and her employees."[8] It seemed these women were all experiencing different forms of being "cancelled." In their ambitious journey to the top, they were accused of engaging in harmful and biased behavior—and in this era of racial reckoning, they were now being held accountable. (It's important to clarify that the three women mentioned have all moved on to new positions.)

At the time, I was leading the coaching division of Inspire Justice, a sister organization to my company. I coached many of these business celebs like the ones mentioned and was finding that a big part of my job was supporting them through an accountability process to understand where they'd caused harm, how to repair it, and how to lead differently in the future. One of the lessons that became abundantly apparent in this process—and that resonated with my own story—was this: when we are living and leading from a place of pain and chasing ambition no matter the cost, we hurt everyone around us, including ourselves.

We are all prone to making mistakes—even those of us from marginalized groups working for a good cause—because we are all human. Regardless, all of us deserve the dignity of repairing and relearning. This became the ultimate lesson that brought all of my teachings together.

An imbalanced relationship with ambition has caused many of us to trip through this unprecedented moment in history, but the justice movements of the last couple of decades—from the Arab Spring and #MeToo to the social justice uprisings of 2020 and climate activism to the current workplace revolution—are shattering delusions. Just not fast enough. We know we need a power shift and to lead differently. We are in a global "stop moment" where we are being asked to pause and examine how we lead because it is no longer working—and never really has.

I know you're tired of your relationship to growth being so fraught. I know you wish another way was possible—and I believe there is. Ambition never means exchanging our sense of self for success. Our visions should never involve exploiting others to achieve our desires. If we have to convince ourselves that our bodies are the collateral damage necessary for our dreams to become a reality, it's not the work and life meant for us.

If you're a woman struggling within the delusion of corporate feminism, an immigrant grappling with the pitfalls of the American Dream, or any other marginalized person with a vision trying to navigate the system, the ambition trap will too often find you. We want to grow, move to the next level, and have the life we desire, but often the cost is too great, and we don't realize it until we've footed the bill. The price of admission can no longer be so great for us.

Some days it may feel like we're taking a step backward, but I believe we are in a moment of realignment. We need a new paradigm for advancement. That's what I am mapping out for you in this book.

Imagine having the crystal-clarity of knowing your purpose and how to honor it in the most fulfilling way.

Imagine releasing the hustle, the chase, and the grind—for good.

Imagine never again feeling the interminable agony of having to force yourself into a workplace not designed for you to thrive.

Imagine not having to compel your body and mind to work at an unsustainable pace.

Imagine your ambition unfolding from a place of purpose and not pain.

My hope with *The Ambition Trap* is to give you the tools to finally honor your growth in a viable way so you can contribute for more than just a season. I wrote this book for you and anyone else who breaks the traditional leadership mold, who followed the shoulds and have-tos only to realize that happiness does not live there. It is for every compassionate soul who feels a burning desire to lead with greater empathy, equity, and respect than those before them. This work is also for all our allies who see what's broken and aspire to support change.

Only when we've done the work on ourselves can we be healthy leaders for others. Only when we've reconciled our own relationship to ambition and freed ourselves from the trap can we help others live freely, too. Let's unearth that triumph together—our time is now.

PART I

Why Your Relationship to Ambition Isn't Working

Chapter 1.

PAINFUL AMBITION VERSUS PURPOSEFUL AMBITION

Ambition is a powerful force. The power of
ambition turns hopeful wishes into reality.
It leads you on the right course to the good life.
Legitimate ambition says, "I only want
something at the service of others, not at the
expense of others."

—JIM ROHN, *The Power of Ambition*[1]

Many of the women I worked with at the height of the
2020 social justice uprisings did harm to themselves
and others because they were leading from a wound
and navigating unfair circumstances. I've been that person. Maybe
you have, too. There are few spots at the top for women and even
fewer for women of color and those living at other intersections.
We are taught to fight to be the best and to compete against our
sisters because the outside world tells us there isn't enough to go
around. Then we are asked to grow at unsustainable paces that
have us cut essential corners. And because we're approaching it all

from a place of not-enoughness or pain, we can't avoid the inevitable pitfalls.

Many of us think that to continue to matter and feel worthy, we must be the fastest, the best, the most notable. But the real trap is believing that. The trap is believing that we are competing to summit the mountain. There is no mountain that we're all on together—only our own personal karmic mountain. It turns out that most of us are chasing our goals from a place of pain—that is the dominant paradigm. But imagine what could be possible in this world if instead we confronted our dreams from a place of purpose.

My client Eve is an influential executive at one of the world's largest biotech companies. An award-winning college soccer player, she brought that same competitive nature to her career. She was hardwired to achieve and succeed regardless of the cost to herself or her teammates. And it worked. She won several industry accolades and made a ton of money, but she felt she wasn't very well liked. She came to me because she'd gotten "in trouble" with HR for the way she was leading and making those on her team feel. She had even discovered that some of her coworkers were calling her "dragon lady." (Eve is Asian, so don't get me started on the racism here.)

When I first met with Eve, I asked her to tell me more about her life to get a sense of how she got here. Through choked-back tears, she shared how, growing up, she had been in foster care and was passed around from family to family. One of the ways she learned to create safety for herself was by outworking others. At her office, she was the first to arrive and the last to depart. She was relentless in her drive to make her projects successful, squeezing every last drop of productivity out of herself and those she managed. As a result, her team made a beeline for human resources to share how much unreasonable pressure she placed on them. They were also quick to mention her harsh communication style that made them feel like expendable resources, not people she respected.

As we explored this more in our sessions, it became clear to me that Eve's desire to succeed was a survival tactic driven by her big, nagging abandonment wound, the source of which was the foster care system she had been raised in. She was convinced that if she worked hard enough, scooped up all the lofty distinctions, and was "the most successful," she would be loved. And if she consistently performed at that high a level, no one would ever leave her. Ironically, it was the way she was showing up to attain that success that ultimately drove people away. When we started to explore that wound together, it was like she suddenly saw her whole life differently.

THE PITFALLS OF PAINFUL AMBITION

Most of us only know ambition in a dysfunctional sense: a relentless desire to succeed, regardless of the cost. *For me to win, someone else must lose,* we think. But that's not ambition in and of itself. Ambition is natural and neutral. In its purest form, it's a desire for more life. It's a wish to unfold, evolve, and flourish. Grass wants to grow; trees like to stretch toward the sun; we all want to thrive. The essence of all living beings is to be motivated for more, and as humans, we're the only species that has a choice in how we direct that advancement. Where things go sideways is when our striving begins to cost us and others our health, relationships, peace of mind, and sense of self. This isn't ambition in its neutral, natural form, but in its most painful.

Painful ambition is the voracious desire to advance, regardless of the cost to ourselves or those around us. It has a few trademarks:

You are unaware of systems that shape our ambition: You are unconscious of the systems that have shaped you and the people around you. You believe we all have equal opportunities to get where we want to go.

You have a narrow mindset:

- You fear failure. You are perfectionistic and unforgiving of flaws in yourself and others.

- You think in black-and-white or either-or ways.

- You have a tendency to live from your limiting beliefs. You lead with judgment.

- You are coming from a place of scarcity.

- You are driven by a need to be seen, heard, and validated by others. You depend on external validation.

You are driven to win no matter the cost: You have a desire to win and succeed for acclaim, or to be liked, and a need to be the best. You chase success based on feelings of inadequacy. You make choices based on the shoulds.

You focus on individualism and hoarding power: You are all about the self and shining as an individual. You believe acclaim and resources are scarce or for the select few, so you amass them for yourself.

You instrumentalize yourself: You overuse your mind and body to get ahead. You dehumanize yourself and others through this intense way of working. You are self-sacrificing.

You practice toxic positivity: You perpetually seek happiness only, avoiding or denying challenging emotions.

You have self-imposed urgency: You move at an unsustainable pace to prove yourself and your efficiency. You move based on fear, inciting panic in yourself and others.

Most of us believe that embodying these characteristics means we're being ambitious. But what we're actually displaying is painful ambition. Keep in mind that this is not an all-or-nothing proposition. We might fall into the trap of painful ambition in times of stress or when we're around others who embody the same qualities, but we very rarely live in painful ambition all the time. And it's uncommon to take on all the attributes at once. Usually, there are one or two traits that plague us the most. We'll explore this more later in this chapter.

IDENTIFYING YOUR CORE WOUNDS

What is behind our insatiable desire to succeed? For most of us, it's a longing to feel loved, valued, and worthy—though there is often a giant chasm between us and that feeling. That chasm is the core wound, one of the drivers of painful ambition. In its simplest terms, the core wound is an aggrieved yet unconscious part of us originating from distressing moments in our formative years. These moments lead us to cement certain beliefs about ourselves—like *I must work hard to be loved*—that now perpetually drive our thoughts and actions and further reinforce these negative beliefs in an endless cycle.

I remember in the first few years of my career, I was so spent by my desire to achieve that I could barely keep up. I would often think to myself, *Can't I just want a little less or be happy where I am?*

The answer to that question was always an emphatic *no*, because where there is metaphorical hunger in our lives, it's the giant hidden wound that keeps us voracious for more. Usually, that craving is so deep that no amount of success, money, food, alcohol, or expensive objects will ever fill the void. If we're not wise to it, that hunger keeps us hustling in a particular role—seeking externally what we need to find internally. Eve's abandonment wound was so great, and her desire to win so vast, that she attracted many painful encounters—from ill-fitting jobs to challenging relationships. Her desire to be seen, be loved, and feel worthy drew her to roles where she would have to work hard, because in her upbringing, she learned that status and awards created a degree of safety and control. She sought out opportunities where the challenges matched her wounds.

In her book *Heal Your Wounds and Find Your True Self*, Lise Bourbeau posits that there are five core wounds that we all experience in our lifetime: rejection, abandonment, humiliation, betrayal, injustice.[2] Let's take a look at each.

> **Rejection:** You felt dismissed and not accepted as a child. Maybe your caregivers were often busy, waving you away and leaving you to care for yourself. Perhaps it felt like your needs didn't fully matter and like there wasn't true connection between you and your caregivers.

> **Abandonment:** You felt discarded as a child and fear being neglected as an adult—including by yourself. The abandonment wound is usually connected with those who felt a deep sense of loneliness as a child. Maybe your caregivers worked a lot, traveled often, or were absent due to divorce. As a result, you felt deserted and fear this happening again.

Humiliation: You felt one or more of your caregivers were ashamed of you. There was an underlying feeling that it was impossible to feel joyful or to feel safe in your joy. You have a fundamental fear of being shamed. Perhaps your caregivers were embarrassed by your physical attributes, such as your weight. There may have been a constant attempt to "fix" you—which just induced more pain and shame. As you age, there is often a fear of being seen due to concern that you will be shamed again.

Betrayal: You experienced feelings of disappointment and fractured trust around your caregivers. You might feel that your caregivers did not live up to expectations. Maybe your caregivers often overpromised but were unable to deliver, leaving you feeling like you couldn't rely on them. Perhaps they missed birthdays, important events, or chose work and other people over you.

Injustice: You feel your individuality in childhood was restrained. You likely had a negative response from a caregiver in connection with your unique personality. Bourbeau defines justice as the "appreciation, acknowledgment and respect of the rights and merit of any individual."[3] Thus when we feel unappreciated for our true selves, we don't feel respected or like we're receiving what we truly deserve. Maybe your parents ridiculed your vivacious, high-energy nature and to this day you don't feel like people get you, which feels unfair.

You may have read through the list and felt like more than one of the wounds resonated. In fact, many of us may have one, two, or all five wounds at play in our lives in varying degrees. Some may even go hand in hand. For instance, you might have felt abandoned and therefore also feel a degree of rejection. I haven't met anyone (yet) who embodies none of the core wounds. So, if you've read the list once and none resonate, sit with it for a bit and revisit it at a later time.

One pattern I've noticed is that the bigger the desire to be seen—to have all the money and achievements without a real why—the bigger the wound is.

Now, I'm not saying that we shouldn't want wealth or accolades. You should get to have everything you desire in this world! In fact, we need more wealthy historically excluded people so we can drive change. The shift I'm talking about here is around our intent: whether our reason for striving is driven by an attempt to fill the voids of our core wounds or by our deep-seated purpose and sense of self.

TAKING OFF THE MASK

Each core wound comes with a corresponding "mask," or a particular reaction molded as a result of the initial wounding experience. Somewhere in childhood, we learn about shame, guilt, fear, and judgment, and it stops feeling safe to be ourselves. We internalize that certain qualities are favorable, and others are less so. According to Bourbeau, we "create a new personality to become what others want [us] to be."[4] This becomes our entire identity as we live with this mask day in and day out. It's not necessarily because our parents were harmful (though, for some of us, they were). This is a very human right of passage. The journey of this lifetime is one of shedding the masks and protective layers and feeling safe enough to come home to ourselves.

Let's look at the masks that correspond with each of the core wounds.

WOUND	MASK
Rejection You felt dismissed and not accepted as a child.	*Withdrawal* You feel a need to escape and run away from people and experiences that bring discomfort. You are avoidant.
Abandonment You felt discarded as a child and fear being neglected as an adult—including by yourself. You likely grew up with a deep sense of loneliness.	*Dependence* You're emotionally reliant on partners and your closest circle and feel like you cannot manage on your own.
Humiliation You felt that one or more of your caregivers were ashamed of you. There was an underlying feeling that it was impossible to feel joyful or safe in that joy.	*Masochism* You put others' needs before your own; you are overly helpful. You feel guilty about experiencing pleasure. You can be a martyr.
Betrayal You experienced feelings of disappointment and fractured trust from your caregivers. You feel they did not live up to expectations.	*Control* You feel a need to control everything around you. You find it challenging to trust others and easier to do things yourself.
Injustice You felt your individuality in childhood was restrained. You likely had a negative response from a caregiver in connection with your unique personality. You felt unappreciated for your true self and like you didn't receive what you truly deserved.	*Rigidity* You feel a need to live in a perfect world, with no space for pain or discomfort. You choose to work hard to block your sensitivity and are highly demanding of yourself.[5]

Ultimately, we can wear these masks forever, which gets in the way of our desired intentions—or we can take them off by doing the work of healing our core wounds. This is what Alana realized when she came to work with me.

A longtime client of mine based in Chicago, Alana is loving, generous, accomplished, well liked, and happily married with two great kids. But when we first started working together, she felt deeply anxious. In our consult call, she recalled tales of tokenism and her former workplace showing her off at recruiting events as their highest-achieving woman at the firm. She had since left that practice and was set to take another job but didn't want to "make the same mistakes." Her former tendencies to people-please, blur her boundaries, and be codependent had left her burned out, bummed out, and in a bit of an existential crisis. Alana had a strong desire to do more connected and meaningful work.

The first exercise I do when working with clients is called the Milestones Exercise. I ask them to tell me the story of their lives based on ten to fifteen experiences encapsulating what they see as peaks (the high highs), pits (the low lows), and pivotal moments (big moments of change). (If you have thirty minutes, try this out for yourself.) Through their storytelling, I get a sense of who they are and how they view their story and core wounds. As Alana vulnerably shared both celebratory and painful moments with me, it became clear that her core wounds were abandonment, humiliation, and betrayal, partly stemming from her parents' divorce. As Alana recalls, when they had to decide on custody, her dad "gave [her] up without a fight." This solidified her belief that she wasn't "good enough," and unless she tried super hard and pleased everyone, she'd always be abandoned. In her mind, at that very moment,

Alana decided to use her assets to be the best. Because if she was the smartest and fastest, she couldn't be ignored or disregarded. People would have to choose her. And so, for thirty-five years after that experience, Alana slogged away under the masks of control and masochism, sacrificing her health and happiness to prove that she was unsurpassed, and in turn was lovable and worthy.

The irony is, when we contort ourselves so other people will choose us, we abandon ourselves. It wasn't until Alana reached the very pinnacle of her career that she realized none of this was making her happy, or actually making her feel "good enough." There weren't enough awards, words of affirmation, bonuses, or elevated titles that could heal this core wound. That would require repairing the original injury through inner child work.

Exercise:
Identify Your Core Wounds

1. In a series of ten bullet points, write the story of your life chronologically. Identify which bullet points are peaks (high points), pits (low points), and pivotal moments (moments of big change).

2. What do you notice about your narrative?

3. Do you see any indications around your core wounds? From the list on page 11, which core wound(s) and resulting mask(s) resonate with you most? Where do you see them in action in your life?

4. Jot down five challenging experiences from the last few years of your life. Do you see any recurrent themes? Do you see any connection to your wounds and masks?

5. Visit aminaaltai.com/bookresources to download a daily meditation to heal your core wound. Practice this meditation for the next thirty days and journal on your experience after each meditation.

THE RIPPLE EFFECTS OF PAINFUL AMBITION

When unaddressed and unchecked, our painful ambition cannot only hurt us but can hurt others, especially if you're in a position of power. Have you ever been accused of not being a team player? Has your perfectionism driven you and the people around you to grueling lengths? Have you prioritized a desire to succeed over the people in your life?

Many of us, like my client Nicole, aren't initially aware that our painful ambition is affecting others until it costs us our reputation and relationships. Nicole was a brilliant professional speaker who toured the country giving uplifting talks to the masses. As a queer feminist and big LGBTQIA+ advocate, she told stories we don't often hear, accustomed to speaking out on edgy topics and areas of womanhood that are often relegated to the shadows. But one day she was accused of ableism and various microaggressions against her colleagues with disabilities and ejected from her role.

When we started our work together, Nicole felt a deep sense of shame that was so burdensome we could scarcely unpack it. She had prided herself on being a well-meaning social justice advocate hell-bent on uplifting marginalized people, particularly at work. How could she have perpetuated the very microaggressions she spoke out against? And to people she cared about in demographics she routinely prioritized?

We started by doing an exercise on self-awareness. I asked Nicole to list three to five challenging experiences she had faced over the last few years. As we chatted through them, her wounds as well as a few themes started to emerge. The sense of betrayal she felt in childhood manifested in her control wound, which was on full display at work. She felt the need to micromanage projects and had a tendency to push her own body to the limit to do so. As a result, she had little compassion for others when it came to their physical and mental well-being. She also had a "pull yourself up by your bootstraps" mentality, not realizing that working harder exacerbates illness and disability for many people. And she preferred to collaborate with others in the organization who had a similar painful relationship to ambition. As a result, she would often leave her disabled colleagues off projects, and refer to their contributions as "cute," further belittling them. In her painful relationship to ambition, Nicole had inadvertently become ableist in her behaviors.

Together, Nicole and I started to explore the difference between intention and impact. We made a list of how she *intended* to lead and what the resulting *impact* was. In some cases, they were aligned, like when she intended to uplift the LGBTQIA+ community and created a supportive employee resource group at the office. And in other cases, the impact of her intention was hurtful and harmful to those she worked with. For example, though she aimed to treat everyone equitably, because she hadn't done enough unconscious bias work, she actually didn't know how to acknowledge that we all have different ways of working and may require different resources to get things done.

Nicole eventually graduated from this work, was able to repair harm with most of those she'd hurt, and learned to lead a whole other way when she started work on her new venture. Instead of operating from a place of painful ambition, she now honored her body's needs and worked toward healing her core wounds and releasing her micromanaging ways. She started to embody purposeful ambition.

EMBRACING PURPOSEFUL AMBITION

So what does it look like to move from painful to purposeful ambition? Engaging in a purposeful relationship with ambition requires us to address our core wounds and shift the orientation of our desire for more. When we operate from a place of purposeful ambition, our growth is no longer driven by a stinging wound. Instead, we've tapped into our intrinsic purpose and are living in a way that has a positive impact on both ourselves and the world around us. We've stopped trying to make life happen to compensate for our pain, and instead are unfolding from a place of wholeness.

In many ways, stepping into purposeful ambition might feel like we are meeting ourselves for the very first time. Many of us unknowingly construct our whole lives around our wounds; in fact, we're often celebrated for them. If we didn't take a physical, emotional, or spiritual "hit" for it, we would likely keep hiding behind them. I know I might have. If it weren't for my health crisis, I may have kept going the way that I was, overworking from a place of not-enoughness. This "hit" is the universe inviting us into a new way of being—it's a way of saying *Stop. What you're doing isn't working anymore and likely never worked in the first place.* This is the moment when we get to put the mask down and peel off the layers of protection. This is when we get to heal that inner child so we can build our lives from the fullness of our true selves versus living and leading from an aching wound. This right here is where circumstances change for the better.

In my work as a coach, I have had the opportunity to support some of the most legendary people of our time, and I have found that it is abundantly clear when leaders advance from a space of *purposeful* ambition versus one of *painful* ambition. Purposeful ambition is pure and honest. And when our ambition is nurtured from this place, it's a healing force for good.

In part II of this book, we'll learn how to move from painful to purposeful ambition. But for now, let's examine what purposeful ambition looks like.

> *You question systems that shape our ambition:* Instead of being unaware of the systems and ideologies that have molded us, you question them. You recognize that the starting line is not the same for us all.

> *You have an expansive mindset:*

> - You realize that each opportunity in our lives is a chance to grow and that perfection is a myth.
> - You question your limiting beliefs.
> - You lead with vulnerability and compassion.
> - You are centered in abundance
> - You actively work to validate and honor yourself. You depend on internal validation.

> *You are driven by purpose:* Instead of being focused on just winning no matter the cost, you have a desire to connect to purpose, have a positive impact, and change

what's broken, and an eagerness to grow from a place of wholeness. You make choices based on alignment.

You are focused on collaboration and using your gifts to help the world: You understand and leverage your gifts for the greater good instead of being focused on the competition. You are all about collaboration, diversity, equity, and community.

You honor your needs: You are in loving collaboration with your mind and body. You center your care and the care of your community. You do not instrumentalize yourself.

You practice contentment: You welcome all emotions and experiences and focus on equanimity, rejecting toxic positivity.

You take aligned action:

- You move at the speed of trust. You are conscious of deadlines and dependencies but honor the people and processes it takes to create great work.

- You prioritize psychological safety over speed and fear.

Now let's look at the differences between purposeful and painful ambition.

THE PURPOSEFUL AMBITION FRAMEWORK

(This framework was inspired by Dr. Tema Okun and Kenneth Jones's work on the bias of professionalism standards.[6] You may find other people are also talking about our relationship to ambition. I'm happy to see reframing ambition is a pervasive cultural conversation.)[7]

PURPOSEFUL AMBITION: A CONSCIOUS RELATIONSHIP WITH AMBITION	PAINFUL AMBITION: AN UNCONSCIOUS RELATIONSHIP WITH AMBITION
Questioning systems that shape our ambition	Unaware of the systems that shape our ambition
An expansive mindset	A narrow mindset
Driven by purpose	Driven by winning no matter the cost
Focused on collaboration and using your gifts to help the world	Focused on individualism and hoarding power
Honoring your needs	Instrumentalizing yourself and others
Contentment-based	Living in toxic positivity
Take aligned action	Self-imposed urgency

Looking at this chart and thinking about the ways in which you might be operating from a place of painful ambition, you might find it a little confronting. *Am I just a big ol' mess who's doing everything wrong?* But you should never feel shame if you've been living in painful ambition, because we've all been there. There was likely a time in your life during which the trademarks of painful ambition served you. The great news is that humans are highly adaptable and we can learn to change these behaviors with just a little bit of conscious daily practice. My goal is to invite you into a new, more supportive paradigm, and to help you unearth where you might be living and leading from pain versus a place of wholeness.

Exercise:
Identify Painful Versus Purposeful Ambition

1. Which qualities of painful ambition do you find yourself embodying?

2. In which areas of your life do you find yourself living more in painful ambition (i.e., work, friendships, sports)?

3. Are there particular conditions that tip you into painful ambition (i.e., stress, feeling short on time, imposter syndrome)?

4. What qualities of purposeful ambition do you find yourself embodying?

5. What conditions support you coming from that place (i.e., psychological safety, compassionate people around you, taking good care of yourself)?

6. What did you learn or notice about yourself from this section?

⚶

Fewer things in life are more confusing than working so hard to get where you want to go, only to arrive there and feel like it's an even deeper rock bottom.

I know you are done with the hardship. I know you are exasperated that the world around you has not always supported your choices and way of being, and how that has fostered a painful relationship with ambition. I know you are tired of getting in your own way. I know you are drained by the constant chasing, forcing, and hustling. I see you. I feel you. I am you. And here is what I know: when it comes to healing our relationship to ambition and living a life that we (collectively) desire, you need to take what is working against you—like your mindset or your wounds—and use it as fuel, energy, and an opening to make a change. As one of my spiritual teachers once told me, "We must use the contrast to refine the vision."

For those of us with marginalized identities who've been sold a bill of goods about success and our dreams in a system not designed for us to thrive: I see you. We want to advance and prosper and have our wildest dreams realized—but in the world we live in the cost is often too great, and we often don't grasp this until it's too late. The price of entry for a "successful life" can no longer be so high. Now it's on us to reevaluate our relationship to ambition and the spaces we've created, and to show those coming behind us a new way forward.

Chapter Summary

- Each of us has core wounds from childhood. We create corresponding masks to hide the initial injuries. These wounds are often fueling our desire for growth.

- Ambition is neutral and natural. In its simplest terms it's a desire for more life. When ambition is driven by our core wounds, we tip into painful ambition. When ambition is connected to our purpose, we embody purposeful ambition.

- There are unspoken rules in society about who gets to be ambitious, and it's usually cis-het able-bodied white males.

Chapter 2.

MINDSETS THAT DISRUPT OUR UNFOLDING

It's never rude to interrupt your false-self.

—Jeff Brown, *Ascending with Both Feet on the Ground*[1]

The Swiss psychiatrist and psychologist Carl Jung once said, "When an inner situation is not made conscious, it happens outside, as fate."[2] I often think about how this dynamic plays out with our ambition. From our initial core wounds of the psyche, all sorts of stories and beliefs can form. Some set us up to achieve our dreams, but most tend to get in the way of our intentions. This operating system is running in the background of our minds, directing our choices and influencing our thoughts—and we're usually not aware of it. And because we're not conscious of it, these beliefs steer our lives in a certain direction that we're resigning to happenstance.

My friend and colleague Khilaal is a physician and well-known activist. He immigrated to the US from Malaysia when he was eight years old. Like me, he had a dad who was a doctor, and in his family, the only worthy professions were law, medicine, or engineering. So, like the good kid that Khilaal was, he went to medical school. He stifled his real dreams and true self to get through residency and make his parents proud. It wasn't until a very dark day, standing on the window ledge of his Manhattan apartment staring at the cold cement below, tears streaming down his face as he seriously contemplated ending his life, when he realized just how unconscious his choices had been. He was living for everyone else but himself, and he could no longer bear the excruciating pain of it all.

Thankfully, grace intervened and Khilaal managed to peel himself away from that ledge, but not without being changed forever. He vowed to look at all the ways he was not being true to himself, and to write a new story for his life.

This is a painful example but an important one. Most of my clients, and perhaps many of us, feel low-grade malaise, frustration, or disappointment over how their careers and personal lives have turned out. But sometimes the discontent becomes so deep, it takes them to the edge, because the unconscious beliefs we have about our careers and lives can present themselves as fate. If we believe ambition means growth no matter the cost, we will do whatever it takes to get ahead. Or we will tolerate poor treatment from others and less than we deserve.

The words of celebrity life coach Tony Gaskins have always stuck with me: "You teach people how to treat you by what you allow, what you stop, and what you reinforce."[3] Many of the people I coach find that their challenges are intensified because they are not teaching people how to treat them. They tolerate being underpaid even if they are overqualified and doing more work than their counterparts because they don't *believe* they can ask for more. They tolerate being under-supported because they *believe* asking for help may prove they are fallible. They tolerate verbal and emotional abuse because they *believe* if they push back, there will be harmful retaliation. And most of us tolerate all of these things because we're afraid not to, and we think it is the cost of entry to an ambitious life. But we are the ones who end up taking a hit for it. Shouldn't work, the place where we spend the majority of our lives, feel good rather than be something we just tolerate?

Carrying the weight of certain beliefs keeps us from creating a healthy relationship to ambition. On the other hand, if we believe ambition means growth at the service of others, we can guide our thoughts, actions, and experiences in a more purposeful way. This is why, when it comes to creating the great work of our lives, we want to get clear on the unconscious programming that's been driving us.

"Unconscious" being the operative word.

THE MINDSET WHEEL: HOW BELIEFS
TRANSFORM OUR REALITY

The first step is to learn how this programming works: our beliefs govern our thoughts, our thoughts guide our actions, our actions produce our experiences, and our experiences reinforce our beliefs. This progression is what is known as the mindset wheel. The diagram comes from Rha Goddess's work in her book *The Calling*.[4]

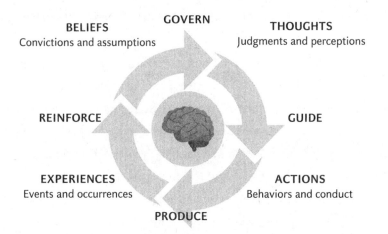

For example, if I don't believe that people like me can be success-ful, that is going to show up in thoughts like *What's the point of try-ing? People like me never succeed.* These thoughts will manifest in my actions, or lack thereof: If I don't believe I can get the job, I likely won't even apply. But because I don't apply, I don't get the job. And all of that together will create my reality of feeling stuck in the same old career, resigned to the same old fate. And round and round we go in an endless feedback loop. See how important our beliefs are?

Where we get tripped up is that more often than not, our be-liefs are derived from someone or something else's belief systems that we've adopted as our own—whether that's our familial up-bringing, cultural imprints, past trauma, or stereotypes (more on this in a minute). Unfortunately, these beliefs tend to be limiting and negative, all thanks to our cognitive predisposition for negative information to outweigh positive information in our brains, other-wise known as "negativity bias."

For example, let's say I've adopted the limiting belief that *women of color can't be well supported in leadership* (which was one of my old limiting beliefs that I learned in corporate America), and I have an experience where someone reinforces that through a major lack of resources and funding. Even if hordes of people back me, because of negativity bias, I'll obsess over the one area I'm being under-supported in and won't believe that I'm actually getting what I need. That belief can then get in the way of me thriving as a leader. When we feel like our desire for more is met with negativity, some of us have a tendency to want to prove ourselves. And few impulses are as destructive.

Many beliefs we've absorbed (whether cultural or familial) also reinforce something called "upper limits," a term coined by psychologist Gay Hendricks in his book *The Big Leap* to describe the arbitrary ceilings we create for ourselves based on limiting beliefs and stories. They usually show up in one of four ways:

- "Feeling fundamentally flawed"—like something is wrong with us deep down inside so we can't achieve what we want because we're intrinsically unable[5]

- "Disloyalty and abandonment"—like if we claim our bigness, we are being disloyal to those we love and somehow abandoning them[6]

- "Believing that more success brings a bigger burden"—either that we'll be a bigger burden or experience more burdens ourselves as a result of having more[7]

- "The crime of outshining"—if we shine brightly, we will outshine someone else and make them look bad[8]

Shifting our beliefs out of these negative, limiting scripts can change our reality, how we feel, and our relationship to ambition. But first it can be really challenging because our brains have been trained to zero in on the negative stories. So for every negative belief we have, we need three to five positive ones to feel even.[9] For example, if the limiting belief is "I'm not good enough to be chosen for this job," a reframe might be:

- I beat out ten other candidates to get the final interview.
- I've done this job before and received an award for my contributions to the field.
- Two recruiters contacted me and said I would be perfect for this career.

Shifting our negativity bias isn't about toxic positivity, however—which is the belief that no matter how dire or difficult a situation is, you should maintain an upbeat mindset. It's about inviting our brains to see the fullness of the situation. It's about looking for the positive, even when the negative is true. It's about both/and thinking.

HOW TRAUMA SHAPES OUR BELIEFS

If you've had traumatic experiences, the mindset cycle may not actually work for you. Trauma affects several areas of the brain, including the prefrontal cortex, amygdala, and limbic system, often leaving survivors in a constant state of reactivity. This can make it difficult to move forward without the support of a therapist or specific interventions.[10] The profound impact that trauma has on the brain and body can significantly influence how we work and live.

One of my clients, Stella, grew up in rural France with great instability. It was typical for Stella to miss meals because there wasn't enough food in the house. On several occasions, she had to move abruptly because her parents couldn't afford the rent, and eventually she started living with her grandmother. School became her safe space. She felt it was the only place in the world where there was consistency, where she was able to get out what she put in. So she put her head down and worked hard, knowing she'd one day make it out of her challenging family home.

And she did. Stella got into the London School of Economics, became an investment banker, and never looked back—that is, until her work "fate" caught up with her. Because she was brilliant and a consummate hard worker, Stella quickly rose to the top. Her firm celebrated her as their highest-achieving woman employee. But she didn't feel happy. Instead, she felt she couldn't be herself at work. She has a wicked sense of humor and a deep love of the esoteric but didn't feel like she could share any of that. Instead, she felt she had to show up a certain way to be accepted—and that way certainly wasn't who she truly was.

But because she never wanted to be pushed out of her home again, Stella did whatever it took to stay in her role. The story that she was telling herself, which had been shaped by trauma, was that if she was anyone but the good-girl hard worker, she'd get fired and end up on the streets like her parents. So she exhibited people-pleasing behaviors to avoid that potential outcome, even at the expense of her own sense of self. Essentially, she had operated in a fawn response for her entire career. Eventually, there was a tipping point. Trying to be "acceptable" took too great a toll, and Stella decided she was no longer willing to live that way and quit and took that time off to work with a trauma therapist.

I want to take a moment to acknowledge how challenging it is to come out of our survival patterns. We do not perpetuate these behaviors because there's something wrong with us or because we're not smart enough to choose something else. Ultimately, we adopted these coping mechanisms because they supported us in some way. As children, they might have protected us from the wrath of our caregivers or some other form of harm. But as we become adults, they can often hinder us more than help us.

When it comes to transitioning from unconscious behaviors to a more aligned reality, many of us don't believe we can have something better, or that something better even exists. That's why, to live the dream for our work and our lives, creating supportive and possibility-focused beliefs is of the utmost importance. Here's the great news though: Through present-moment awareness, mindfulness, and reframing tools, we can shift those pesky negative beliefs. Because when we don't, those biases can fuel our wounds and warp our reality. Try the following exercise to get started.

Exercise:
Create New Beliefs

1. When it comes to your career, relationship to money, and achieving your dreams, what are the stories you tell yourself? Make a list and try to be as exhaustive as possible, and note where there might be a limiting belief.

2. Close your eyes and notice your breath for a few breath cycles. Visualize the first time you believed this story to be true. Where did this belief come from? (For example, maybe when you were in the third grade, you raised your hand to answer a question and everyone laughed at you. You felt embarrassed. In that moment, you decided you weren't good enough and shouldn't even bother trying.)

3. For every limiting belief you wrote down, ask yourself, "Is this really true?"

4. If you answered yes, we want to debunk those beliefs by citing three examples to the contrary. I know this process can be tricky. Our brains see the world in a particular way based on our lived experience, and we often have to start small and dig deep to find evidence that these old stories aren't true. Even the smallest example can help us change our beliefs. Read these new beliefs every day until they become your default.

BRINGING OUR SHADOWS TO LIGHT

One way to identify your limiting beliefs is to pay attention to your shadows. Do you find that certain people, words, or experiences cause you to bristle? Have you ever been terrified that someone will find something out about you and reject you? Maybe you get worried people will think you aren't smart enough, that you don't have the correct qualifications or right background for the position, or that you are somehow a failure. Or you feel triggered by other people's attributes, like their candor or ability to set boundaries, and it gets in the way of you feeling competent in your career. And perhaps all of this causes you to wear a mask at work (and everywhere else, for that matter).

Once again, we are back to Carl Jung. Jung was the first to introduce the concept of shadows, or the "dark" sides of our personalities we hide in order to stay safe, lovable, and acceptable to our communities, families, and society at large. Debbie Ford, author of *The Dark Side of the Light Chasers*, says the shadow "contains all the parts of ourselves that we have tried to hide or deny."[11] Our shadows can look like selfishness, incompetence, or self-importance.

We are so afraid that anyone will find out about these traits of ours that we bury and hide them at all costs. Paying attention to these shadows can help us identify the subconscious beliefs we have about ourselves.

One way to detect our shadows is to observe what we judge in others, as this is usually what we judge in ourselves. For example, my client Andrea was a supertalented marketing executive who never felt good enough. She had a strong desire to be the best, but she felt like she could never say those words out loud because it would make her seem "gross" and "competitive," as she put it. Though she had achieved award-winning results for her company, she was quiet about her success and kept her head down, hoping that hard work alone would get her noticed. When she was passed over for a promotion, which was given to one of her less experienced but much more vocal peers, Andrea was seething. She resented this person. When she came to work with me, she told me all about how "full of themself" this person was. They were often overheard celebrating their achievements and telling everyone how great their results were, Andrea said, which really rubbed her the wrong way. After listening to a few stories like this, I had a hunch that there might be a shadow at play there—and it was the idea of being boastful.

But where do our shadows come from? There are several ways they can originate, the first being through the insecurities that were reinforced by our families, communities, and cultures. For instance, I come from a long line of hard workers. My great-grandparents on my mother's side were coal miners who did backbreaking work just to survive; all of them succumbed to injury or illness they experienced from working in the mines. My inspiring entrepreneurial grandmother, whom I loved so much, worked in her business until she was eighty-six; my mother had to physically remove her from the office because she was still going to work despite suffering from dementia. Laziness is so taboo in my family that we work through chemo, grief, miscarriages, divorce, and even degenerative brain disease. If I came home exhausted from a hard day's work, I was praised. If I stayed home or didn't work as hard, I was called "selfish" and "lazy." Picking up on the idea that laziness was the worst thing in the world, I decided to work twice as hard to prove to people that I wasn't this way. And just like that, laziness became my shadow and caused an over-rotation into hard work. It was like this dirty word had a hold over me, but I wasn't conscious of it. If someone had asked me when I was fourteen years old why I was working so hard, I would have said something like, *Because I want to succeed.* Unbeknownst to me, there was a big, wounded shadow living right in the center of all of my doing, fueling my desire for bigness and growth.

For a lot of us, our shadows are unfortunately also a reflection of how the world thinks of us and our worthiness, and they can reflect painful stereotypes. Take my client Natasha. She is a brilliant and extremely well-educated Black woman working in the legal field, but her shadow is being "ignorant." This might sound surprising coming from someone who is clearly clever and has as many credentials as she does. As we unpacked her shadow, Natasha realized some of her feelings of inadequacy were rooted in anti-Black stereotypes that have been ingrained in American history since before the Civil War. No wonder Natasha had this shadow, and thus over-rotated to show the world how brainy she is.

Many of us experience stereotyping based on our age, race, gender, size, immigration status, ability, sexual orientation, religious beliefs, and more. We're barraged by the stereotype of "the

angry Black woman." Or that Asian employees are "more reserved." Or that employees who live in larger bodies are "less motivated." Or that older employees are "out of touch with technology."
Or that millennials are "entitled." Many ambitious underrepresented people hold the belief that parts of us are wrong and so we
overcorrect to amplify a counter-quality, but in doing so we trap
ourselves in inauthenticity and fear. All of this can lead to the creation of a shadow and can affect how authentically we allow ourselves to show up at work.

The reality is, we all contain the full spectrum of human emotions and traits. There are moments when you will get angry and
lash out, moments when you won't be able to speak up even if you
want to, moments when your actions might rub someone the wrong
way. The trouble comes when our shadows have a hold over us. I
abhorred the word "lazy" so much that I put on this whole performance so as never to be perceived this way. I also came to judge it in
others because, as I shared with Andrea, what we are judging in
others, we are also judging in ourselves. This cycle of judging can
trickle out and have wide-ranging societal consequences. According to Christopher Perry of the Society of Analytical Psychology,
the shadow "fuels prejudice between minority groups or countries
and can spark off anything between an interpersonal row and a
major war."[12] When people project their unacknowledged shadow
aspects onto others, especially those from different groups, it can
result in baseless negative beliefs and prejudice. These projected
negativities can, over time, escalate into major conflict.

Here's the problem with burying our shadows: When we fail to
acknowledge or integrate our shadows, we continue patterns that
interrupt our own growth and interpersonal relationships, all while
perpetuating painful ambition because it often drives a narrow

mindset, competition, or limiting beliefs. When we deny the truth of who we are, the daily stress of being someone else and wearing a partial mask takes its toll, and, like a volcano, we will erupt in one way or another. For me, that eruption was my initial health crisis. For you, it might be quitting a job out of the blue as a reaction to your manager, grappling with debilitating panic attacks, or engaging in self-sabotaging behaviors such as binge drinking. Living into a performance is exhausting. Only when we integrate our shadow can we be real and whole and thrive authentically.

In *The Dark Side of the Light Chasers*, Ford says:

> When we suppress any feeling or impulse, we are also suppressing its polar opposite. . . . If we deny our fear, we minimize our courage. If we deny our greed, we also reduce our generosity.[13]

In other words, what we don't own, owns us. When we realize that all our traits—from our laziness to our selfishness—serve us in some way, we stop labeling parts of ourselves as "wrong" and others as "right." We integrate. And as Ford says, when we integrate our shadows, we become whole:

> We live under the impression that in order for something to be divine it has to be perfect. We are mistaken. In fact, the exact opposite is true. To be divine is to be whole and to be whole is to be everything.[14]

Integrating our shadow involves welcoming our "dark" parts instead of rejecting or shaming them. When helping my clients through the process of integration, it's important to see the other side of the shadow—that it's not all bad. A great place to start is by looking up the origins of a word. For example, when I started to do the work to integrate my "lazy" shadow, I looked up its etymology. It comes from the German "lasich," meaning "languid." It suddenly clicked for me: What's wrong with being slow and relaxed? Humans weren't designed to be in perpetual motion. In fact, most humans need to slow down and relax every night. In this stillness our bodies repair themselves and get rid of harmful toxins. Resting is an important part of living and of our purposeful ambition. It's in the pauses that we see the bigger picture and our deeper why.

Working with my client Andrea, the ambitious marketing exec I mentioned a few pages ago, we launched headfirst into an exercise to find and integrate her shadow, inspired by Debbie Ford's work. First, I share a list of adjectives and ask my clients to jot down the ones that feel the most painful or uncomfortable to them. Then we distill those words into a few common themes.

After doing this with Andrea, we saw that in her family system, being humble was applauded while celebrating oneself was looked down upon as "gross" and "braggy." Therefore, while growing up, Andrea inhabited the idea that downplaying one's gifts and contributions was somehow more noble. She kept her head down and worked hard but never once celebrated her success, and that way of being served her—until it didn't. (This is true for many women. We're told not to be overly confident because it's off-putting, only further perpetuating our shadows and resulting in lost promotions, skipped title bumps, and missed pay raises.) When Andrea was passed over for the promotion and found herself burned out and bummed out from working so hard without recognition, she was ready to do things differently.

Let's explore your shadow in the exercise below, which I've created based on Ford's work in *The Dark Side of the Light Chasers*.

Exercise:
Find and Integrate Your Shadow

1. What's the one thing you fear others might discover about you?

2. What are the top five things you judge in other people? What are you judging them for? Is there a pattern?

3. Make a list of three people who rub you the wrong way. What qualities do they embody that are triggering to you?

4. Are you starting to see a pattern around what you judge in others and in yourself? Where might you have learned that these qualities were "bad" or "taboo"?

5. How is this shadow creating dysfunction with your ambition or at work? For instance, has it kept you from getting a promotion or created a tough dynamic with your team?

6. To go deeper and further integrate your shadow, listen to the meditation I've created for you and see what insights come up. Visit aminaaltai.com/bookresources.

UNDOING CODEPENDENCY AT WORK

There is one particular pattern that I see over and over again that interrupts a healthy relationship to ambition in a big way, and that is codependency and codependent thinking as it pertains to work.

What is codependency? Melody Beattie, author of *Codependent No More*, originally defined a codependent person as "one who has let another person's behavior affect him or her and who is obsessed with controlling that person's behavior."[15] Many of my clients don't relate to Beattie's definition of codependency because they are a unique brand of codependent. They are what psycho-therapist and author Terri Cole refers to as "high-functioning co-dependents." In her book *Too Much: A Guide to Breaking the Cycle of High-Functioning Codependency*, Cole offers a more complete definition. It's marked by being "overly invested in the feeling states, the decisions, the outcomes and the circumstances of the people in your life to the detriment of your own internal peace and emotional/financial well-being."[16] The patterns of codependency include self-sacrifice, a focus on others' needs, suppression of one's own emotions, and attempts to control or fix other people's problems—all of which can disconnect us from our unique abilities and keep us tethered to self-sacrifice.

One tricky aspect of codependency is that it can feel rewarding. It feels nice to help people! It feels good to be needed! But when we lean in too hard, we abandon ourselves—and that is a trademark of painful ambition. Back in my agency days, I used to regularly sacri-fice my own needs for my employees and clients. I'd pull all-nighters to meet a client's unreasonable deadline. I'd expand my scope of work without charging them more. I would give them everything I had, even what I didn't have. It left me resentful and overworked, but I wasn't yet able to see my role in this dynamic. Instead, I was obsessed with fixing my business partner's unconventional ways. He was the risk-loving albeit brilliant visionary, and I was the solid good-girl caretaker. I figured if I focused on changing his ways, things would run smoothly. But we were in a codependent dance where he would break things, I would fix them, and we'd continue that cycle without anything ever changing.

You might not be pulling all-nighters, but you could have a co-dependent relationship with work if you're sourcing your esteem entirely from it. This can look like having the following beliefs:

- *I'm not allowed to say no:* Maybe you say yes to everything because you feel responsible for how other people feel, which can go along with a tendency to do anything to help shift uncomfortable feelings, like anger and disappointment. When we aren't holding a firm boundary, we can become depleted, resentful, and frustrated.

- *I need to be in control:* Perhaps you feel a need to manage others—to make everything okay for them or to control the outcome. You may feel a lack of personal empowerment, and so resort to monitoring those closest to you.

- *I need external validation to feel worthy:* Do you feel the need for approval from others? Do you people-please to avoid conflict and stay in people's good graces? This can also look like needing to be right much of the time. In being "right," we validate that we deserve to be here, and our existence is therefore "right."

- *I'm not allowed to put myself first:* For many codependents, self-sacrifice is a way of life. Does feeling needed feel close enough to being loved that you sometimes settle for it? When we act in this way over time, it can greatly erode our sense of self.

- *I need to be perfect:* Many codependents at work equate their worthiness with perfect output. Do you wait to put work out until it's perfect? Do you hold on to ideas, waiting for the "right" timing (which never seems to come)? Our pursuit of perfection can result in a range of issues such as an overly critical inner voice, constant judgment of others, rigid black-and-white thinking, overworking, aversion to new experiences, fear of failure, rumination, and feelings of anxiety and depression.

Ultimately, at the root of these behaviors is shame—the shame of not feeling good enough, smart enough, educated enough, quick enough, or ____ enough (insert whichever word resonates with you). Researcher, author, and social worker Brené Brown has a great definition of shame: "that warm feeling that washes over us, making us feel small, flawed, and never good enough."[17]

But there is nothing "wrong" with us—there is everything right with us. We simply need to keep an eye out for these patterns so we can put down control, caretaking, and other behaviors weighing us down, and instead anchor our work in our purpose. If we don't, we may end up unconsciously sabotaging ourselves.

Exercise:
Release Codependency and Establish Boundaries at Work

1. Of the codependent traits shared in this section, which ones resonate with you (if any)?

2. Where do you find yourself defaulting into codependent behaviors? Are there specific relationships where those behaviors are more present? Why do you think that is the case?

3. When we stay stuck in a role or a dynamic, it's often because we're getting something out of that role or dynamic. What are you getting out of yours? How might you shift?

4. Where do you feel shame at work? Where do you feel "less than" or "not good enough"?

5. What is the story you're telling yourself about this thing you're ashamed of?

6. What boundaries do you need to establish in your life to help you separate your identity from your work? Think about your physical, emotional, and time boundaries.

7. What will establishing these boundaries make possible?

SUBCONSCIOUS SABOTAGE: OUR ATTEMPT TO FEEL SAFE

Sometimes, when we haven't fully addressed the core limiting beliefs and wounds driving our ambition, they culminate in self-sabotaging behaviors. We may end up going out of our way to be destructive because subconsciously it doesn't feel safe or attainable to have what we want. Gay Hendricks, author of *The Big Leap*, has a great analogy for this:

> Each of us has an inner thermostat setting that determines how much love, success, and creativity we allow ourselves to enjoy. When we exceed our inner thermostat setting, we will often do something to sabotage ourselves, causing us to drop back into the old, familiar zone where we feel secure.[18]

And that's where "sub-c sab," as I lovingly refer to subconscious sabotage, comes in.

There are many ways you can subconsciously sabotage yourself:

- *Doing things to 99 percent completion, dropping the ball on the last 1 percent, and saying, "See, it didn't work."* Notice how sneaky self-sabotage can be? On the outside, it might look like you're doing *everything* you can. But internally, you're pumping the brakes just before the finish line. And you might think that the last 1 percent won't make a difference, but it does. Think of 100-meter runners in the Olympics. If they stopped running one meter before the finish line, the outcome would be wildly different.

- *Allowing yourself to stay in confusion by not asking for clarification when you don't understand something.* If the path to your dreams is unclear, how can it be your fault?

- *Perpetuating feelings of overwhelm (usually due to porous boundaries), so you don't do the work you were born to do.* You may unconsciously take on too much of other people's work, so you stay bogged down rather than focusing on what is most meaningful to you.

- *Sidetracking yourself with things that aren't relevant to your dreams.* You may often busy yourself with tasks that don't move the needle, so you appear hard at work but not in ways that get you to your dream.

- *Overthinking things and then not taking action.* Overanalyzing our path forward can often look like we're being strategic and thinking through all obstacles. But it's often a smokescreen or tactic to stay in our swirling minds and never get to action.

But why do we sabotage ourselves? Supposedly we want the thing we said we wanted. If we really desire the dream, why are we trying to take ourselves out? In my experience, I think we sabotage for two reasons. First, as we've learned so far, there is some unmet need at the subconscious level, like a need for safety, love, or belonging. And second, we're terrified of our own bigness.

Fear of our own bigness is so pervasive. We want to feel positive, hopeful, and empowered, but at the same time, when we take up more space and are more visible to the world around us, we become more susceptible to potential disruption. That's because the world often has feelings about our growth that aren't always positive, especially as historically excluded people. So we hide as a way to stay safe. In fact, subconscious sabotage could also be referred to as "safety restoration," because we're often engaging in it when our nervous systems don't feel safe enough to hold the experiences we desire. So our brilliant minds and bodies will work hand in hand to restore us to our comfortable old ways—and our comfortable old ways are often illustrative of our painful ambition.

That's what happened to my client Mariah, a celebrated CEO of a regional bank. While on a retreat together, she disclosed to me she was having near-daily panic attacks. The bank had hired her for her impeccable track record and because they wanted to platform a woman of color. But Mariah was sabotaging big-time. She delayed writing articles and op-eds, she didn't prep for board meetings, and she'd stumble over her talking points—it was starting to become a problem. Clearly Mariah was accomplished and had everything she needed to thrive. So what was happening? She was trying to keep herself safe.

When we realized what was occurring, we examined the source of this behavior. Growing up, Mariah's mom had narcissistic personality disorder. Mariah was often on the receiving end of her mother's rage—and if you have ever experienced narcissistic rage, you know just how terrifying it feels. When her mother would unleash her anger on her, Mariah would often feel "like she was going to die." So, somewhere in her brain, she clung to the idea that she should not take up too much space, for if she did, people would come for her the way her mother did, and she would feel that same dying sensation. Her brain literally set up the connection that being seen and taking up too much space equals death, so she sabotaged to stay safe until, through our work, she could consciously see what she was doing.

In order to expand into the truest versions of ourselves, we have to feel safe enough to take risks and claim our power. But in many ways, nothing is scarier, particularly for historically excluded people. Many of the clients I work with are afraid to take up too much of the spotlight for fear of backlash. And that backlash is so real and often far harsher than the feedback received by folks with more dominant identities. Thus, our nervous system needs to regulate accordingly to be able to support us in that bigness. But when the alternative is living a life we don't desire and that is not aligned with our values, we want to get acquainted with that fear, examine our trauma, and prime our nervous system to meet our bigness.

Exercise:
Where Are You Subconsciously Self-Sabotaging?

1. Over the last few years, were there any big career moments where you engaged in behavior to sabotage yourself? Perhaps that looked like excessive judgment, control, addiction, or inaction.

2. In those scenarios, what do you think made you want to bring yourself back to "safety"? What were you feeling?

3. When you think about taking up space and standing in your bigness, what fears arise? How do you feel in your body? Are there particular places in your body that you feel sensations? If you gave those sensations a voice, what would they say?

4. What needs to happen for you to feel safer as you rise to your next level?

5. Visit aminaaltai.com/bookresources for an exercise to support your nervous system and build internal safety.

⚜

All the subconscious beliefs I've outlined in this chapter can lead us far, far away from the real dream for our work and our lives—and when left unchecked, can create a very unhealthy relationship with ambition, indeed. But they often also serve a purpose. In chapter 1 of this book, I shared one of my favorite lines from my spiritual teacher, who suggested that any time we hit a bump in the road, "We must use the contrast to refine the vision." In our case, the contrast is any belief that is not desirable or causes friction in us. The good thing about contrast is that it allows us to see where we missed the mark, where we got in our own way, or where the world around us did not support us. Equipped with this information, we can adjust our aim again. Codependency, limiting beliefs, a lack of boundaries, and the resulting challenges can serve as a compass that allows us to further hone our dreams and ambitions.

Of course, we don't operate in a vacuum. In addition to our core wounds and our beliefs, there are systemic forces at play that keep us stuck in a painful relationship with ambition—which we'll explore in the following chapter.

Chapter Summary

- Our mindsets can set us up for success or get in the way of every desire. But the good news is, our brains are malleable so we can shift our thinking!

- All of us have a negativity bias so we have to put extra emphasis on the positive to crowd out our propensity to focus on the challenging.

- We all have areas of our lives that we're tolerating. But tolerating life is expensive and often costs us what we really want.

- Shadows are the parts of ourselves that we've tried to hide or deny. We all have them and sometimes they are reinforced through stereotypes.

- Codependency isn't just for romantic relationships— we can show up with those same traits at work and it can really interrupt our fulfillment.

- Subconscious sabotage is when we unknowingly engage in behaviors that undermine our success. Sometimes it's a form of safety restoration.

Chapter 3.

THE SYSTEMS AND IDEOLOGIES THAT KEEP US TRAPPED

We were raised to believe that if we worked hard
enough, we could win the system—of American
capitalism and meritocracy—or at least live
comfortably within it. But something
happened. . . . We looked up from our work and
realized, there's no winning the system when the
system itself is broken.

—ANNE HELEN PETERSEN, *Can't Even: How
Millennials Became the Burnout Generation*[1]

Puja was an accessories designer in New York City. She was
the only woman of color above the manager level and had
fought hard to get there. She was great at her job and loved
doing it because it meant she got to work with brilliant creatives.
But now, fifteen years into her career, it was starting to feel like a
slog. Each season rolled into the next, and Puja never seemed to get
a break. She worked consistent sixty-hour weeks but felt like
"golden handcuffs" kept her there, meaning there were few other

spaces that would pay her so well and grant her the lifestyle she was accustomed to. Plus, her employer kept promising her the title of creative director if she kept up the work, so she hung on and stayed immersed in the hustle. On top of everything, as an Indian American woman working in the somewhat elitist fashion industry that celebrates Eurocentric standards of beauty and professionalism, Puja felt that in order to become as "polished" as those in the space she was operating in, she had to leave some of her real self behind.

But having to push her true self down to adhere to biased standards of professionalism and perform at such a fast pace for so long started to unravel her, and she began drinking as a way to numb the pain. It started as one or two drinks after work with colleagues. Then it turned into drinking while she was working in the evening. Eventually, she was at thirty drinks a week and could barely recognize herself in the mirror. Her wife threatened to leave and begged her to get help. Puja dutifully obliged. And then, one night on the way home from an AA meeting, she stopped at a bar, blacked out, and made it home in the middle of the night.

The next day, hungover and filled with shame, Puja broke down to her wife, finally admitting that her life and relationship to alcohol, work, and unrelenting productivity was untenable. She was burned out from having to present this perfect version of herself at the office and having to work twice as hard to be perceived as worthy as her white peers. Alcohol had become her way to cope. Now she was ready to release the overworking culture that had led to these devastating emotional and physical effects and to get the help she needed.

When we started our work together, we looked for the origin story that led Puja to believe she needed to overwork, tone down her personality, and seek validation from others to matter. We didn't have to look very far. Puja was raised in a low-income immigrant household where she was lauded for her work ethic and placed in advanced classes starting in elementary school. Every day at drop-off, her mom would remind her that if she was the most industrious one in the room, she could have a different life, she could have all the things her family was going without. Puja's teachers celebrated her diligent tendencies, and it made her feel safe and accepted. In her words, she "assumed the stereotype of the 'model minority,'" which suggests that AAPI communities are obedient, hardworking, and law-abiding citizens whose success is attributed to these traits. Being the hardest-working person in the room became her identity.

As we can see through Puja's story, our painful relationship to ambition isn't simply an individual issue. From capitalism telling us our worth is determined by how much we produce, to racism, sexism, ableism, and all the other isms perpetuating the lie that who we are is "less than," there are very real systemic and structural inequities that usher us into painful ambition and keep us stuck there. As much as certain people would like to tell us otherwise, we cannot shift ourselves out of systemic oppression through mindset alone. In order to release ourselves from the ambition trap, we have to become conscious of the systems and dogmas that have ensnared us.

THE ORIGINS OF HUSTLE CULTURE

If you've ever believed that work is your whole life and that you should derive your value and self-worth from perpetually competing through your job and bank account, you've been a victim of hustle culture. A pillar of the girlboss and tech-bro eras, hustle culture is, as journalist Adrian Horton puts it, "the distinctly American, quasi-religious belief system . . . that work is not merely a job but an identity."[2] Hustle culture has cost many of us our relationships and our hobbies, not to mention our physical and mental health—much like Puja.

Unfortunately, we are primed to hustle long before we enter the workforce. Our ideas of overwork are shaped by those around us, from the ways our families and caregivers navigate the world to how our school systems categorize and sort us, especially those of us who are marginalized. School systems are particularly biased in setting certain students up for a life of overworking. From gifted and talented programs that prioritize achievement culture to the inequities between different school districts, we laud overworking and overachieving at an early age without making appropriate resources readily available to all. For example, according to a report by the Education Trust, there are fewer seats offered in advanced classes for schools with a higher percentage of Black and Latino students, and Black and Latino students are often denied seats in those types of classes in more racially diverse schools.[3] From the get-go, we set marginalized groups to be under-resourced, initiating the impulse to work twice as hard and be twice as competitive in order to get half as far.

Hustle is pervasive in marginalized communities. The word "hustle" was used by many Black families through much of the twentieth century to describe what they had to do to make ends meet; in his 1965 memoir, Malcolm X wrote, "Everyone in Harlem needed some kind of hustle to survive."[4] Historically, due to redlining, segregation, workplace discrimination, and bias, many Black employees have had to exert double the effort to achieve only half the progress compared to their white counterparts—many working multiple jobs to get by. Artists like Lil Wayne and Rick Ross rap about hustling, underscoring Black resilience through their lyrics. Song after song reinforces that hustling isn't just cool but is a necessary tool for survival in a system designed to oppress Black Americans.

And then hustling made its way into corporate America's lexicon. In 2015, Uber's famously toxic CEO Travis Kalanick introduced hustle into the company's brand language. His singular desire for Uber was "winning,"[5] a hallmark of painful ambition, so he established one of their company values as "always be hustling," aka "get more done with less, working longer, harder, and smarter, not just two out of three."[6] Uber appropriated the idea of hustle and weaponized it against the very people doing most of the labor—mainly immigrant, BIPOC, and working-class people. In fact, Kalanick himself was caught on camera berating an Uber driver, defending his inequitable tactics. (It's worth noting that after much backlash of its always-on, exploitative culture, Uber reestablished its values in 2017, choosing to release "hustle" from its corporate vernacular.)

Then there was WeWork, the infamous coworking space built by Adam Neumann through questionable business practices and erratic behavior. It wasn't long before his harmful conduct caught up with him, leading to a botched IPO and a troubled exit from the company.[7] But WeWork had already created its own relationship to hustle, with "Hustle Harder" neon signs emblazoned across the Instagrammable spaces, a signature visual of many of its locations.[8]

This use of "hustle" in the corporate context is a form of linguistic appropriation that allows people in power to take what works for them (and capitalism) while discarding the origins of its meaning and the people it pertained to. The problem with this is that it traps many historically excluded people into even more unsustainable and exploitative relationships with work. Many under-represented leaders I work with and talk to feel as if they cannot release the hustle and grind because they are already operating at a deficit. They often ask themselves, *Am I doing enough? Could I be doing more?* And it's usually the very same question their investors and employers are also asking them because of their own unconscious biases.

Ultimately, hustling was—and still is—a reality for many marginalized people in America. When the system isn't designed to support you, sometimes you have to push to make space for yourself and get by financially. But hustling is not sustainable. I think most of us would be happy to renounce our overworking ways. The million-dollar question is, can we afford to?

I believe we can, but it would require a system-wide shift. Why? Because one of the pitfalls of hustle culture is that it creates an environment in which overwork is not only normalized but celebrated—and most harms the ones we need to uplift.

OVERWORKING IS A SYSTEMIC (AND ECONOMIC) PROBLEM

In 2016, overworking killed 745,000 people across the globe by dramatically increasing our risk of stroke and heart disease.[9] Yet as a culture, we've come to glorify it. Those who engage in overwork are viewed as more committed and competent by their organizations.[10] And thanks to the gig economy, as well as the decline of stable work, overwork has become the norm. With the pandemic, Zoom entered many of our homes, inviting our managers into our most intimate spaces and further blurring the boundaries between work and life. As we now depart from the standard workweek and into more "flexible" arrangements, we tip into the 24/7 "rise-and-grind" culture millennials are known for. But clearly, that idea is hurting us. According to a study from Indeed, 52 percent of the US workforce reports being burned out post-pandemic compared to 43 percent pre-pandemic.[11] And a study from MetLife found that millennials are the most burned out of all the generations, giving credence to what author Anne Helen Petersen calls "the burnout generation," with Gen Z following closely behind.[12]

The media frequently presents overwork as an individual decision that can be remedied through greater organization, time management hacks, or one more adaptogenic beverage. However, overwork isn't as simple as personal choice—it's an economic problem.

Increasing economic inequity is one cause of long working hours, even for people higher up the wealth ladder. These days, even those in the C-suite are feeling financially insecure. And this financial instability, particularly in the United States, causes many to overwork, motivated either by the reward of more money or the threat of financial hardship. No matter where we fall on the economic ladder, most of us feel trapped in overworking.

Many of us started our careers around the Great Recession of 2007–2009, one of the worst economic declines in US history. We've also had to navigate rampant social injustices, late-stage capitalism, the glorification of overwork due to hustle and girlboss cultures, and the global pandemic. Petersen explains that "the overarching thing is precarity."[13] This precariousness, that we are one event away from disaster—whether it's losing our jobs, experiencing another recession, or falling ill—takes a huge emotional toll. We are perpetually waiting for the other shoe to drop, and this fear fuels an often unsustainable relationship with ambition—this is a sentiment that I've noted across generations.

There's also a correlation between overworking and trauma. Some of us have had to overwork to survive in a system that only allows certain people to advance in meaningful ways. Others developed a proclivity toward overworking as a result of racial or gender-based trauma at work or school stimulating a propensity to overwork to prove we belong. Countless studies demonstrate the link between addiction and trauma[14]—and overworking *is* a form of addiction, in that it allows us to avoid our feelings of pain or lack of worthiness. If we feel such extreme discomfort in our believed not-enoughness, we may toil away to distract ourselves from the agony we feel on the inside. In lots of ways, the system is designed to take advantage of those feelings of not-enoughness.

But I don't believe that we were born simply to work. Life is an opportunity for us to express the full prism of who we are, to feel joy, discomfort, excitement, and curiosity. To play, to work, to create, to rest, and to recover. To just be. Dutch inspirational speaker Alexander den Heijer says, "You often feel tired, not because you've done too much, but because you've done too little of what sparks a light in you."[15] But sometimes we are tired for both reasons: because we do too little of what actually lights us up *and* because certain systems have obligated us to do too much. As a society, we have also placed great emphasis on working and very little on pacing, rest, and recovery.

To live a life in alignment with our purposeful ambition, rest is as important as action, and pacing and recovery are essential parts of our survival. Did you know there is such a thing as an Olympic sleep coach? Sleep coaches and doctors help high-performance athletes optimize their rest and recovery periods in what is playfully referred to as "sleep doping." Sleep specialist to the USA Weight-lifting team Dr. Jeffrey Durmer puts it so well: "Overtraining syndrome is really not about overtraining, it's about under-recovery. So if you're not recovering enough, your training itself could become a detriment."[16]

This is such a perfect metaphor for our whole lives. We cannot continue to show up for ourselves, the people we love, or our missions if we do not pace ourselves and rest. Yet this moment in time can make that challenging. Unfortunately, we live in an always-on society that was structured to keep most historically excluded people perpetually working. We're also bombarded by stories on social media of what productivity and advancement should look like. Therefore, navigating this moment is like running an ultramarathon. We cannot do it effectively if we do not pace and replenish ourselves along the way. It is in the restful moments that we get to reconnect to the bigger why behind our ambitions.

If you're reading this and feel like there is just no way you can slow down because you cannot afford to, I see you. I really get it. And I want you to understand the why behind your striving so you can start advocating for yourself (and system change) in a bigger way.

Exercise:
Has Overwork Led to Burnout?

1   Have you become pessimistic or defeatist at work? Even toward things you used to deeply care about?

2. Does it require more energy and effort to get to work than it did before? Do you have trouble focusing and getting started each day?

3. Do you have far less patience for your constituents and people you used to care about (clients, team members, managers)?

4. Do you feel drained emotionally and physically? Do you have much less energy to deliver the work you need to?

5. Is it getting harder to focus?

6. How often do you feel overwhelmed by your work and to-dos? (Not often, often, very often.)

7. Do you feel motivated? Have the things that used to drive you become less meaningful?

8. Are you using any avoidance strategies so as not to feel discomfort (e.g., shopping, alcohol, or food)?

9. Are you having physical symptoms like headaches, stomachaches, or changes in sleep or appetite?

10. Do you ever give yourself a hard time for needing to rest or for being in a period of not producing? If yes, why?

11. What do you notice about your experience with hustle and overworking?

THE PAY GAP

Why do so many of us historically excluded people feel a lack of worthiness that tips us into an unsustainable relationship with work to begin with? One of the reasons has to do with how biased financial systems keep us in a cycle of overwork and complicate our relationship to ambition. According to the Global Gender Gap Report 2023, it will be 131 years before we close the gender gap at work, and that timeline has slowed significantly thanks to even more global instability in the past few years.[17] Even in North America, where opportunities are more readily available, it will still take at least fifty-nine years to achieve gender parity.[18] Though there is very little data on pay equity for transgender and non-binary people in corporate America, according to a 2019 Williams Institute analysis, "one in five LGBTQ+ adults in the United States (22%) live in poverty," compared with 16 percent of their straight and cis-gender counterparts.[19]

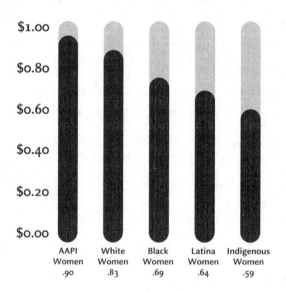

The gender wage gap across race[20]

Throughout our lifetimes, these wage differences can amount to millions. It can be the difference between having savings and not. Between being able to withstand a medical crisis and not. Between living in poverty and not. Women seventy-five and older are more than twice as likely to live in poverty compared to men, and though this is multifactorial, the wage gap doesn't help.[21] Money, in too many cases, *is* freedom. It's the ability to invest in resources. The wage gap can be the difference between being able to pay for childcare and support, so you can rise through the ranks at work if you so choose, and not. The lack of pay parity is just another way certain systems interrupt our success and intercept our ability to grow in a purposeful and harmonious way. My clients and I have all worked extra jobs or taken an additional client to make more money, which has often exacerbated overwork and sometimes even illness.

The dominant narrative used to be that women are not as financially savvy. Common financial advice used to tell women to cut back and make themselves smaller by not buying the latte or the shoes—basically equating us with frivolity. But what if we just paid people equally instead?

CERTAIN MINDSETS ARE ACTUALLY CULTURAL AND SYSTEMIC TRAPS

In addition to the pitfalls of hustle culture, overwork, and financial inequality there are a few beliefs that many of us wrestle with that are more appropriately defined as cultural traps. Let's explore them together.

Imposter Syndrome

When I first came to coaching, I didn't see anyone who looked like me, and I immediately thought that I didn't belong. I felt like a complete imposter, a feeling many of us are all too familiar with.

The term "imposter syndrome" was coined in 1978 by clinical psychologists Dr. Suzanne Imes and Dr. Pauline Rose Clance, who first called it the "imposter phenomenon." Initially, they were studying their female students who had feelings of intellectual phoniness despite their achievements and accolades. When they extended their study to interview 150 exceptionally successful professional women and students, they found that many of them shared these traits. Much of this had to do with representation at the time: it was easy for women in the workplace to look around a room that was predominantly male and make the assumption that they did not belong.[22]

Today, imposter syndrome can happen when we feel we're not like the core or dominant group in our organization—maybe you're the only queer person in your environment, or perhaps the only woman or neurodivergent person. When we feel like we don't belong, we start to question our abilities despite how accomplished we are. Perhaps you've felt the same way? Many of my clients are the first or only historically excluded person in the room. Feeling different from the in-group causes them to question their gifts and sense of belonging. And this happens to the majority of us, as 70 percent of us will have some experience with imposter syndrome in our lifetime.[23]

Here's the problem with imposter syndrome, though: It takes a perfectly human set of behaviors, such as fear and doubt, and pathologizes them into a syndrome, particularly for women. When Imes and Clance conducted their research in the 1970s, they didn't take into account the effects of racism, classism, homophobia, transphobia, or xenophobia on our psyches. Imposter syndrome is not a mindset issue, it's a systemic one.

In an article published in *Harvard Business Review* by Ruchika

Tulshyan and Jodi-Ann Burey, titled "Stop Telling Women They Have Imposter Syndrome," we can see this properly broken down. They say:

1. "Imposter syndrome puts the blame on individuals, without accounting for the historical and cultural contexts that are foundational to how it manifests in both women of color and white women."

2. "Imposter syndrome directs our view toward fixing women at work instead of fixing the places where women work."

3. "Workplaces remain misdirected toward seeking individual solutions for issues disproportionately caused by systems of discrimination and abuses of power."[24]

Going back to when I first started coaching, my feeling of imposter-hood was partly due to my own belief system and partly due to the system I was operating in: being able to take a risk on a second career is a form of privilege that isn't available to everyone. Starting again at the bottom often requires time, money, and resources that are not always ubiquitous for people with marginalized identities. Women—and women of color, in particular—don't often get second chances, and any failure, no matter how "fast and often" or in service of growth, is scrutinized and evaluated in a much more insidious way.[25] Though there is little data and research on this, anecdotally, coaching is understood to be mainly white and female. At the time, coaching was a fledgling industry, and not a lot of people of color could take a risk stepping into it.

Systems of discrimination and abuses of power within those systems are what cause us to question ourselves and lean into a less healthy version of our ambition—and feeling like we don't belong often causes us to work harder to prove ourselves. Focusing only on our own alleged inadequacy is a distraction from the broken system. We need to focus *less* on fixing ourselves and *more* on shifting a broken world. And we cannot have a conversation about historically excluded people and ambition without looking at the systems that have posed the obstructions.

Lack of Psychological Safety

I was once asked to facilitate a conversation between a group of senior female leaders and their CEO at a fintech company. The company wanted to be able to recruit, retain, and nurture more women in leadership, and to do that, they needed to understand what was getting in the way.

In this discussion, we invited women to share openly about their experience at the company. Woman after woman shared stories of sexism, microaggressions, a churn-and-burn culture of long hours at odds with their life outside of the company, and their experiences of being excluded from major deals and accounts. The CEO listened to a handful of personal stories and took notes when other women would nod in affirmation that they had experienced something similar. Midway through our ninety-minute conversation, the CEO said he had a very different view of the organization and hadn't seen any of this happening. In one sentence, he invalidated everyone's experience in the room and undermined their psychological safety. The sharing ended there.

Harvard organizational behavioral scientist Amy C. Edmondson defines psychological safety as "a belief that one will not be punished or humiliated for speaking up with ideas, questions, concerns, or mistakes, and that the team is safe for interpersonal risk-taking."[26] This can look like feeling safe to fully participate in brainstorming because you know you won't be shamed if your ideas aren't perfect, or kindly questioning our peers and even authority if we think a mistake has been made. It may look like being secure enough to ask our manager questions we feel we "should" know the answer to. If you're a manager or lead a team, creating a psychologically safe environment is how you make sure everyone, especially historically excluded people, has an opportunity to contribute and thrive. Too often, organizations lack psychological safety, which perpetuates exclusion, and in my experience, fear lies at the heart of this dynamic.

For those who don't see themselves as part of the dominant ingroup, the absence of psychological safety is even more pronounced. And if we don't feel psychologically safe, and instead are also driven by fear, we inadvertently operate from a place of painful ambition. We cannot have a purposeful relationship with ambition if we're unwilling to look at how we're undermining psychological safety inside of the spaces we create, especially for us historically marginalized people.

The lack of psychological safety we feel at work is usually a direct reflection of the broader lack of psychological safety in the world around us; it's a microcosm of the macrocosm. We have few historically excluded people in our governments creating policies that would keep us safe and thriving. (White men encompass 62 percent of all elected offices, even though they are just 30 percent of the US population.[27]) All of this is reflected back to us in the demographics and policies of our organizations as well. Psychological safety is absent in cultures where people wish to lead with fear— where the prevailing belief is that there is one right way of doing things, a hallmark of painful ambition.

Scarcity Mindset

In her book *The First, The Few, The Only: How Women of Color Can Redefine Power in Corporate America*, Deepa Purushotha-man writes that "the idea of scarcity is the most important mind shift we need to make if we truly want to change traditional defini-tions of power."[28] Scarcity mindsets are perpetuated by people in power to preserve their rank and create infighting among margin-alized groups.

Years ago, I reached out to collaborate with a speaking agency. They were a well-known bureau and secured major talks for thought leaders worldwide. The agency came highly recommended by a female colleague whom I greatly respect, so naturally I thought they would be a strong fit for me. I hopped on the video call and shared my experience, my ethos, and my particular thought leader-ship. At the end of the call, the co-founder thanked me for reaching out and shared that they had just signed another "Middle Eastern woman" and were looking for someone who was "more obviously a person of color." At first I was shocked. I couldn't believe that they were actually saying these words out loud. It felt painful and frus-trating, especially as I was seeing their roster filled with my white peers. I wondered, was there also a quota for cis-het white folks?

When people in positions of power perpetuate the idea that there is only space for one woman of color, one queer person, one person with a disability, etc., it can make us feel like we have to fight everyone else who looks like us to land a spot where we want to be. We also often question ourselves, our impulse being that we're in the wrong. But that is a particularly insidious form of to-kenism, because it perpetuates the idea of scarcity and competition among the very people we want to lift up.

Though we are seeing more historically excluded people in leadership roles, there is still much headway to make. For every hundred men that make it to a manager position, only eighty-seven women are promoted—and for women of color, that number drops to just eighty-two: this discrepancy is called "the broken rung."[29] What ends up happening is an organization that isn't diverse at every level—instead, it more closely resembles a corporate caste system because not enough effort is made to nurture and make space for talent at every rung of the ladder. The reality that we get promoted at lower rates also reinforces this idea of scarcity. And even if we do make it to the top of the ladder, the headwinds we experience— fewer resources, microaggressions, more pushback—are much more severe than our cis-het, able-bodied, white male counterparts,[30] often impacting our tenure and the quality of our experience and making our ambition feel burdensome.

The reality is, there is space for us all. The idea that there isn't room for everyone is a reflection of people's unconscious bias—and is a trap we can easily fall into.

GLASS CLIFFS

As a result of systemically engineered scarcity and tokenism, many historically excluded leaders are now falling—or being pushed— off the "glass cliff." The glass cliff is a situation in which a woman, BIPOC individual, or member of a marginalized group rises to a leadership position in tumultuous or challenging times (like during economic recessions or movements like #MeToo), when the probability of failure is higher than usual, because companies decide they need something or someone different to shake things up.[31] Usually that means they're looking for a leader who isn't the default white male. Thus, women and other underrecognized leaders are appointed during the most challenging moments, end up with fewer resources, and are ultimately pushed off the proverbial cliff.

There's a lot of research that backs this up. For example, studies have found that women are more likely to be placed in leadership positions in general financial and performance downturns.[32] Historically excluded leaders are more likely than their white male peers to be hired at struggling firms, which, again, creates more obstacles to success.[33] The research suggests that we are given less support and less time to demonstrate we can turn things around and when "failure" inevitably happens, we are then replaced by the traditional leaders—aka white men. This idea has been dubbed the "savior effect."[34] However, we wouldn't need to be "saved" if we were given appropriate resources to save ourselves. A lack of resources can lead us to compensate in other ways, ultimately exhausting us through an invitation to prove ourselves, and in that dynamic, we often lose who we are.

My client Emily's last role was as the executive director of a global nonprofit. It was a very well-known organization but long past its heyday—but Emily always loved a revitalization project. When she took on the role, the organization was struggling. They shared some of those challenges in the interview process, but Emily couldn't see the actual data or degree of the difficulties until she officially started the job. On the first day, she learned that the previous ED had wildly mismanaged their funds and they were now at major risk of losing their endowment. Plus, there was a mountain of compliance issues Emily would need to wade through to right the ship. Emily did her best to close that gap and pulled out every tool in her tool kit, only to miss the mark by a wide margin, which eventually led to her being replaced.

She didn't know it then but this was a classic glass cliff moment. They put her, a woman of color, in a tenuous leadership role, gave her very few resources, little to no support from the board, and essentially set her up to fall off the cliff. Emily told me that she had never been the kind of person who thinks *Woe is me!* and she tried her best to make magic happen. But when she couldn't, she mined the experience, trying to understand where she went wrong and what she could have done better: *I should have asked more questions and clarified the financial situation before signing on the dotted line; I should have asked for more resources before agreeing to take on the work; I should have done many things differently.* In hindsight, there were so many red flags, and deep down, she knew that organization wasn't a place she could thrive, but she wanted the executive director title. It was the perfect pitfall. The voice inside her head said, *If I can turn this around, they'll see that I'm worthy,* and she turned herself inside out to try to make it happen. She felt like she needed this last title on her résumé to be taken seriously. And the underdog wounded part of her wanted to be able to steer a course back to stability and make things better for everyone. But there was no way she could make those changes in that system—and she fell into the ambition trap as a result.

The lack of resources and mentorship Emily experienced is common for women and people of color. Women of color are less likely to receive the mentorship and sponsorship needed for advancement.[35] Black male professionals have less access to senior leaders than their white male counterparts.[36] Thanks to the "similar-to-me effect," most leaders tend to lift and mentor folks most similar to them in appearance and way of thinking.[37] Since we have a shortage of Black and historically excluded people in leadership, we then lack the necessary mentorship, interrupting Black and historically excluded people's ability to ascend. And round and round we go.

Our underrepresentation at the top is not due to a lack of ambition—we have it in spades. Black professionals are more ambitious than their white male peers.[38] Women of color are more ambitious than their white female and male colleagues.[39] Our lack of representation in the highest ranks of organizations is not because we don't want to succeed or to rise to leadership positions—we have greater headwinds and far fewer tailwinds.

But it is the system and its inherent bias that has failed us, not us failing as leaders. The glass cliff is a clumsy and superficial way to address a lack of representation and only ends up creating more harm. Few things will warp our relationship to ambition as much as being asked to run a race in half the time with half the tools. It perpetuates a sense of urgency, perfectionism, and overworking that is often hard to intercept or recover from.

The structures we've relied on have let us down, leaving us with two options: to operate in a dysfunctional space that fuels our painful ambition or to take matters into our own hands.

Some of these systems and collective behaviors have driven many marginalized people to entrepreneurship. The pandemic encouraged more women of color to start businesses—not from a place of opportunity, but from a place of necessity. Faced with childcare issues, financial strain, job losses, and perpetually being underpaid and undervalued, many decided to solve these problems for themselves. The absence of vital support in corporate and government systems forced people to create their own more supportive structures. Most corporations haven't done enough work to make space for the rising group of talented, ambitious, and game-changing underrecognized leaders, so many choose to make space for themselves.

⚘

Though systems of oppression are very real and culpable, it is not all doom and gloom. I believe we can operate in an unfair system *and* have the lives we desire while we work toward a different world. Both can be true. This data may be sobering, but I see so much expansion and possibility for us all.

Chapter Summary

———◇———

- Certain ideologies sustain painful ambition, thus painful ambition isn't just an individual issue but a systemic one.

- Hustle culture has been weaponized by corporations to further harm those who need to be most uplifted—historically excluded people.

- Overworking is a systemic issue. We wouldn't be trapped in over-doing if we all had the same starting line. The pay gap is a perfect example of this.

- Systems of discrimination and abuses of power within those systems are what cause us to question ourselves and lean into a less healthy version of our ambition—and feeling like we don't belong often causes us to work harder to prove ourselves.

- Imposter syndrome is not an individual issue. Instead of fixing historically excluded people at work, we need to fix the places historically excluded people work.

- People from marginalized groups face greater headwinds and fewer tailwinds.

- It's not all doom and gloom. I do see the tide slowly turning.

PART II

Embodying Purposeful Ambition

Chapter 4.

HONOR YOUR PURPOSE

Success means we go to sleep at night knowing
that our talents and abilities were used in a way
that served others.

—MARIANNE WILLIAMSON,
A Return to Love[1]

So far, we've spent most of this book exploring the core
wounds, mindsets, and systems that drive us toward painful
ambition. But at the end of the day, we do not have to suc-
cumb to that pain-fueled way of working and striving. We can
make our way forward and achieve our wildest dreams, even after
major setbacks. The first step is to find—then honor—your true
purpose.

But first, what exactly is purpose?

PURPOSE: OUR REASON FOR BEING

In Western cultures, we tend to conflate our purpose with our work—
but they are absolutely not the same. Purpose is how we express our

essence in the most authentic way possible. Your purpose, in its most simplistic form, is your sacred contribution—whether that is to family, community, or the greater good. Our work can be an expression of our purpose, but it doesn't have to be (and often isn't). It's not necessarily about having a brilliant career but about understanding the brilliance that is within us. In fact, certain Indigenous cultures, such as the Laguna Pueblo people, believe that because our existence mirrors nature,[2] we are not here just to make money and change the world, but to be weird and wonderful, just as nature is. To be ourselves, you might say, and bring forth the purest, strangest, and most genuine parts of us and offer them up to others. When our ambition comes from that place, humanity heals.

A lot of us feel weighed down by the idea of purpose. However, our actual purpose is generally quite simple. It's the *expression* of our purpose that really trips us up. Some of us may come to earth to change the world and others may have incarnated this time around to make life better for one person by showing up in kindness, or by bringing more beauty to the planet through their art, music, or generosity. Your purpose can have a far-reaching impact or live a little closer to home; there is no right way to do it. That's why I love author Stephen Cope's definition of purpose—to "bring forth the best that is within us"[3]—because it means your purpose is actually quite straightforward. For example, my purpose is to help people come home to themselves. My dear friend and fellow coach Shirin's purpose is to bring forth joy in every interaction.

When we design our work from a purpose-filled space versus a place of pain, life unfolds so beautifully and so much more is available to us. We feel freedom and fulfillment. Our days are more meaningful. We live in a way that is true to who we are and what we came here for. When many of us think of purpose-driven work we usually envision teachers or someone running an NGO. In actuality, it is any contribution that leverages the best of us. Living in our purpose is our birthright. We should all have the opportunity to contribute the best that is within us, though we don't all get that. However, if and when we do, we can inspire others to do the same and create a ripple effect in the world that changes everything. This is how our purpose is interconnected with others around us. The more we tap into this authentic reason for being, the more chance we have of transforming the systems and structures that repress us and limit our potential.

In this chapter, I want to invite you to be an active co-creator of a better future for all of us by virtue of living your purpose. I'll be talking about purpose within the context of our vocation, since this is a book about being in the right relationship with our ambition as we work, but let me be clear: our purpose is so much bigger than our day job.

Exercise:
Unearth Your Purpose

1. When it comes to your purpose, what does it look like to "bring forth the best that is within" you?

2. What did your soul come here for in this lifetime? Close your eyes and notice your breath for a few breath cycles. Allow the answer to come through without pushing or forcing. If this question feels way too large, try some of the other prompts and come back to this.

3. Take out your journal and fill in the blank: I came to earth to ___ .

4. What do you want to make better for yourself, your family, your community, or the greater good?

5. Once you've looked inward, it may also be helpful to use other tools at your disposal. I love astrology and human design to help clarify purpose as well. You can also visit aminaaltai.com /bookresources for a meditation on unearthing your purpose.

6. Purpose can feel like a really big topic to home in on. If you found the above questions difficult to answer, keep a daily log of where you are "bring[ing] forth the best that is within" you. Check in after a month and notice what themes arise.

Unfortunately, where a lot of us get tripped up is when we confuse purpose with its similar yet wholly different cousins: performance and passion.

PURPOSE OVER PERFORMANCE

Many of us came of age in trophy-winning, degree-obsessed, optimized-performance times. We were taught that if we thrust ourselves into overdrive in pursuit of a noble goal, it meant we were worthy. So we competed in the dance competitions, karate belt ceremonies, and spelling bees without much of a sense of what was for us and what wasn't. Unfortunately, many of us carried these same competitive, performance-driven ways into our careers. We became preoccupied with the title, promotion, and whatever next advancement could be had—and these outward signs of success became our sole reason for striving. In some cases, we've become so consumed with this need to perform that we conflate our achievements with our identity.

But performance, at its root, is an act—one of how well we complete a piece of work or activity. Most of us play out this act our whole lives, until it stops working for us. But a need to accomplish something without knowing our why often results in pure chaos. It leads to imbalance, burnout, and often harm to ourselves and others in order to get to the goal. Remember the girlbosses and tech bros I mentioned earlier?

When we're working and striving from a core wound, most of us become fixated on performance. We want to hit the mark and do a great job, but we generally don't have much sense of why—other than to fill our need for security, safety, and worth. But what we know from hearing my clients' stories in part I is that all the perfect performances and achievements in the world will never make us feel whole. That is internal work we must do on ourselves.

My client Kim is a great example of this. A marketing executive who started her career working with big beauty brands in the consumer packaged-goods space, she was awesome at her job and sold a lot of "shit," as she told me in our first meeting, from mascaras and contour kits to face serums that we surely didn't need more of. She was attuned to making consumers want what she had. She was an "achievement monster" (her words, not mine) and worked long hours, pulling all-nighters to prep for global marketing meetings and ensure her products continued to sell. She was elated whenever she attained a higher revenue for the companies she worked for. Then, at thirty-six, she was diagnosed with thyroid cancer and, suddenly, it all felt kind of pointless. The diagnosis and resulting radiation therapy were grueling. To add insult to injury, the radiation thrust her into early menopause, robbing her of the choice to carry her own children.

Devastated by this experience, Kim was determined to make

meaning of it and set off on a journey to examine everything she was putting into and on her body. Some studies she read suggested that common chemicals in makeup are endocrine disruptors,[4] and even lead to certain types of cancer.[5] After three years of research and working with labs and green chemists, Kim launched her own clean makeup brand. She was committed to educating other people on the potentially harmful chemicals found in our everyday products. Kim felt her purpose was to share a new way of being. She channeled that into her career by helping consumers make better choices for themselves and the planet so they wouldn't have to end up sick like she did. "Less shit, more solutions," she jokingly said in our final session.

In her former jobs she chased the goals set out for her in order to feel worthy. In her new venture, she was committed to using her own pain to change what was broken in the beauty industry. Her work was having a positive impact on the people and world around her. She was making choices based on alignment. In her previous career, Kim was consumed by performance. This time around, she was captivated by purpose.

WHY PASSION ISN'T ENOUGH

Sometimes some of us might mistake passion for purpose. In fact, much of our cultural conversation around work is centered on the importance of passion. But have you heard the aphorism "Do what you love, and you'll never work a day in your life" and thought, *This doesn't apply to me*? Many of us are passionate about our work, but the truth is, work doesn't always, well, work for us. In fact, the fetishization of lovable work is often what sets us up to fail. Once we follow our passion, we believe, everything else will fall into place—our relationships, our finances, our well-being, and our happiness. And therein lies the problem.

The truth is, focusing on passion alone positions us to fizzle out fast. A Deloitte study on burnout found that 87 percent of workers are passionate about their jobs, but a whopping 64 percent of those same people feel regularly stressed, shattering the myth that if we're passionate about our jobs we won't burn out and all else will be solved.[6] I've seen many people who were so passionate about their profession that they never took time off, and ultimately crashed and burned. Or who had to shutter their businesses because they loved their work so much, they practically gave it away. Erin Cech, author of *The Trouble with Passion: How Searching for Fulfillment at Work Fosters Inequality*, calls this the "passion principle": prioritizing personally fulfilling work, even if it means compromising on job security or a substantial salary.[7]

When you focus on passion alone and are willing to take significant financial risks in the name of passion, it's a sign that whatever you're doing may not be sustainable. And when work isn't sustainable, we break down, get sick, or quit. Unsustainable work that is fueled by passion alone is a trademark of painful ambition. Besides, the reality is that a career based on passion by itself isn't viable for everyone. Those who come from affluent and upper-middle-class backgrounds are better positioned and have the necessary social connections and financial safety nets—such as inheritances or supportive parents covering expenses during unpaid internships—to secure employment that aligns with their passion.

This is why I'm an advocate for purpose over passion. Aligning with your purpose instead of just your passion allows you to honor your gifts in a way that is practical and nurturing, not exploitative. This is the entry point into a healthier relationship with ambition.

EXPRESSING YOUR PURPOSE

As I shared before, your purpose can be simple. However, the process of expressing your purpose can take some time and tends to be the space that is more fraught for most of us. But there are a few ways for us to begin that process together.

Create a Constellation

The North Star, officially named Polaris, is the brightest star in the Northern Hemisphere toward where Earth's axis points. It appears to hold almost completely still, which is why in many cultures it has come to symbolize truth. Our purpose is a lot like our North Star; it's the truth we follow. But in this day and age, it can feel like a lot of pressure to choose a singular North Star. Many areas will spark your interest and inspire you to leverage your gifts. And especially with greater access to information, more of us can develop new skills and reach more people. Allow your true self to be fully expressed by casting off the idea that the expression of our purpose is a singular North Star.

I like how my fellow teacher of purpose and author of *Applied Empathy* Michael Ventura describes it when he says we build our lives "around a constellation as opposed to a singular north star . . . those points of light in your life that are helping you to realize your full and complete self." The constellation then becomes a "wayfinding tool."[8] We utilize these points of light and connect them to the story of us and what we're here to share. Using a constellation to guide us in the direction of who we are called to be is a much more generous approach than the pressure of one brightly burning North Star.

For example, I started my career in marketing, which gave me a solid business foundation. It clarified for me that I wanted to work with underrecognized founders and leaders. After my health crisis, I was called to center well-being in my work because I knew how crucial it was for us to thrive. All of those stars in my constellation led me here.

For you, navigating your constellation may look like being drawn to a career in private equity, which then ushers you toward the work of closing the gender wage gap, which then becomes a movement to support working mothers through policy change. We move from one brightly burning spot to another and we allow our direction to continually unfold.

Draft a Mission Statement

When it comes to following your constellation of purpose, it's helpful to also have a mission statement. Our mission statement is our personal objective and includes the vehicles through which we plan to realize our constellation of purpose. For example:

- As I shared earlier, *my purpose* is to help people come home to themselves.

- My *mission* is to help historically excluded people unearth their purpose, peace, and prosperity, which are a means to coming home to yourself.

- I do that through business and career coaching, speaking, courses, my podcast, and this book, which are my *vehicles*.

Let me give you another example. My friend Shirin, whom I mentioned earlier, identifies her purpose as *bringing forth joy in every interaction*. Her mission is to *transform people through joy*, and she is accomplishing that through her vehicles of *coaching, podcasting, and teaching*. She delivered on the same purpose in her previous career as an opera singer and is now doing it as a coach. Her purpose and mission remained true—it's the vehicles that evolved over time, and the same is true for me.

See how purpose, mission, and vehicles play together?

Now I want you to get clear on how your purpose translates into a mission and vehicles. Use the exercise below to help. Before you begin, though, I want to note that this is big stuff, and sometimes these questions can feel impossible to answer. So take a first pass and keep the stakes low. Our mission and vehicles get honed and evolve over a lifetime, not in a single sitting.

Exercise:
Define Your Mission and Vehicles

1. What are you on a mission to do? What is your objective? Fill in the blank: I am on a mission to ____ .

2. Fill in the blank: I want to lead us toward a world where ____ is possible. (This can be in the context of family, community, or the greater good.)

3. How might you be the perfect person to lead us toward that?

4. Get clear on your why. Why is this mission so important to you? What would it make possible in your life and in the world around you?

5. Is this in alignment with your purposeful ambition? Is any of this coming from a place of pain? If yes, how might you shift your orientation?

6. What vehicles enable you to deliver on your mission and purpose? It could be your day job, an entrepreneurial venture, a podcast, a series of workshops, a speaking tour . . . literally anything.

Live Directionally

As we start to identify and follow our purpose, we should allow the expression of it to evolve as we ourselves evolve. We are not static, so why should the way we share our purpose be? One of my dear friends and fellow coaches Megan Hellerer, who was Alexandria Ocasio-Cortez's career coach, calls this living *directionally* versus *destinationally.*

Living destinationally looks like pursuing one specific goal: to get the job, make a certain amount of money, buy a house, or achieve a certain status. Everything we do is with the aim to get closer to that destination. Living directionally, on the other hand, means pursuing what captivates us in any given moment, even as it changes. Instead of pursuing a destination, we allow ourselves to go inch by inch into new opportunities, following our own internal guidance every step of the way. From our current vantage point, we may only see a few steps in front of us. But as we take those next steps, a few more appear, and a few more. Each action we take reveals where to place our footing next. This is why living directionally is so important. If we give ourselves permission to shift along the way, we might arrive in a wildly different place than what we thought possible.

My client Linda is the embodiment of living directionally. Her purpose is to help people feel at ease, which she did in her previous career as an interior designer and now, too, as a nutritionist. When she first shifted her career from design to nutrition, she didn't think she wanted to work one-on-one with people. She wanted to be a course creator and thought leader, and she didn't see herself straying from that. But as she started developing and testing her offering—something that necessitated being one-on-one with clients—she realized how much she loved the depth of one-on-one work. It felt good in her body. Her inner GPS was pointing her toward something she'd previously thought wasn't for her. Living destinationally, Linda would have stuck to her original plan and forgotten all about one-on-one work. But in living directionally, she ended up pivoting her vehicles and feeling much more fulfilled as a result.

We live in a world that doesn't always make us feel like we're allowed to change our minds. We honor the tenacious folks who stick things out all the way to the end, no matter how misaligned those things may be with our purpose. We celebrate grit, resolve, and persistence. But what is the point of all of that if it is in violation of who we are, what we want, and what will make the world better?

I'd prefer to be misunderstood than to reduce myself to something I'm not. So, as you move from star to star and get clear on your mission and vehicles, give yourself permission to evaluate your alignment at every interval. There is major power in releasing what isn't for us, no matter how far we are down the path.

LIVING OUT YOUR PURPOSE: THE ALIGNED LEADERSHIP FRAMEWORK

Now that we're closer to knowing what purpose is and isn't and how we can start to define it, I want to share a tool to help you identify how to embody it through your work. Whenever I help clients unearth their unique purpose, I take them through a process called the Aligned Leadership framework. This framework helps you determine how you can best *express* your purpose by serving as a metric through which you weigh new jobs or business ideas to ensure they are aligned with who you are and where you want to go. So whether you need to make a decision about your next big career move or are trying to determine if your latest passion should be your grand entrepreneurial venture or simply a hobby, this framework will clarify what is for you and would provide the most fulfillment, and what is not and won't. This is your litmus test.

Now you might be thinking, *Didn't you just give us a framework to decide if we're in alignment with purposeful ambition?* Though the Purposeful Ambition and Aligned Leadership frameworks work hand in hand, they're different. Purposeful ambition ensures that our desire for growth is coming from the most true and authentic parts of us. The Aligned Leadership framework ensures that however we bring things to life is the most harmonious. Purposeful ambition is about *you*. The Aligned Leadership framework ensures that whatever opportunities come your way *match* the real you.

Let's say you get a call from a recruiter offering you a fabulous job across the country. It's going to double your salary and give you the next title you were after. Awesome! Only thing is, you're passionate about the environment and this company is not. They create a ton of environmental waste. But you tell yourself, *The salary is so good, maybe I can make an exception.* To decide if this is a *heck yes* or a *hell no*, you would run this opportunity through the five pillars of the Aligned Leadership framework:

- Is this aligned with my gifts? *Yes.*

- Is this aligned with what I value? *No, it is not aligned with my value of honoring our environment.*

- Is this aligned with what brings me contentment? *No, because I'm going to be in daily conflict with my values.*

- Is this aligned with what I want to impact? *Somewhat, because more money means more change. But the broader environmental impact is a no.*

- Is this aligned with what I need to bring my vision to life? *It meets my salary needs but not my mission.*

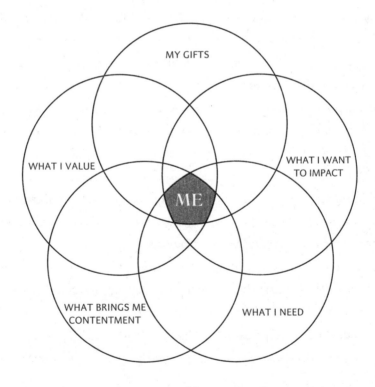

Ultimately, through the Aligned Leadership framework, you would see that this new opportunity is actually in violation of your values and the impact you want to have—so even though it looks shiny, it is not aligned with who you are and what you need.

We'll be diving into each aspect of the Aligned Leadership framework in the coming chapters, but for now, let's look at how each works.

Our Gifts

The Aligned Leadership framework centers our gifts because to work in a way that feels like a salve for the soul, really expresses who we are, and makes the change we want to see in the world, we need to leverage the best of us. We all have a unique form of brilliance, a rare talent or ability that is specific to us and that we came to this planet to share. For some of us, it's power skills like deep listening, empathy, and communication. For others, it might be a more tangible skill, such as playing the trombone or being really good at physics. A lot of us are taught that genius is for a select few, but I believe that's a patriarchal myth that supports some people and aids in the oppression of others. When we bring our brilliance to the world, we can finally drop the hustle and grind and work with our natural flow. We'll go into this more in the following chapter.

Our Impact

Our impact is how our actions, projects, and policies affect people, communities, and the environment. Impact is part of the framework because it's how we know that our work is truly connected to our purpose. Purposeful ambition is wanting something at the service of others, not at their expense. Thus, evaluating our impact is integral.

Amazing shifts can take place if we all care about impact—and these changes are happening right now. From #MeToo to Black Lives Matter, from convening marches on climate change, to demanding our workplaces make efforts to be more inclusive, to challenging stakeholder capitalism, we are the generations creating real change. Millennials and Gen Z count climate change as a top-two concern.[9] They want their work to impact the world, with 63 percent of Gen Zers saying their employers must share their values.[10] And racial justice is a top priority, with 60 percent of Gen Z and 56 percent of millennials acknowledging that systemic racism is widespread.[11]

The latest data suggests both generations have expressed deep concern about the state of the world and are trying to balance their fight for change with the demands of their everyday lives. We're juggling volunteering and our work lives, relationships, and self-care. We are also putting our money where our mouths are—spending money with brands whose values and impact align with ours. In fact, almost 75 percent of Gen Zers believe that being politically and socially active is important to their identity and shaping the future of the world.[12] It's heartening to see that we acknowledge what is broken, and we're ready to drive change.

Our Needs

Honoring our needs must be part of the litmus test because it ensures sustainability. I cannot tell you how many clients I've had over the years who have tried to force an opportunity that wasn't going to meet their needs. They'll say, *But Amina, I get to work for this amazing NGO, and I'll be doing so much good. Gifts, check. Impact, check. Needs, well . . . it's half the salary I need but they're offering me a free parking space.* No! That does not alignment make. When we are worn out and bedraggled because we can barely make ends meet, we cannot show up for our purpose in a sustained way. It's a surefire bet for burnout.

Many of my clients find it really challenging to honor their needs, as so many of us have been indoctrinated to believe that suffering is noble, and were taught that we need to put our needs behind others'. But that is an unsupportive approach to ambition. Kelly Diels, teacher and coach to culture makers, once said, "If we are not taking care of the feminist running the business, are we really running a feminist business?" This really stuck with me and applies to all historically excluded leaders in whatever way we're honoring our purpose. If we aren't taking care of ourselves and supporting our needs, we lose our ability to do this work and feel good in our lives. And if the work fails to exist because we didn't take care of ourselves, have we really made a difference? When we prioritize our needs, we're not just doing it for ourselves. We're setting a precedent for everyone who is navigating life with a similar lived experience.

Thankfully, the tide is slowly turning. Gen Zers are more likely to take a personal day for their menstrual cycle and consider "quiet quitting" as part of their self-care.[13] They refuse to exchange their well-being and sense of self for their work. They are taking a stand for their needs in a way that previous generations did not or were not able to do. In terms of honoring our needs, I am much more aligned with this take. A healthy relationship with ambition is marked by sustainability—and sustainability is a by-product of honoring our needs.

The goal, though, isn't only to take care of ourselves so we can enhance our productivity and output—it's to honor our needs because we deserve that as humans.

Which brings me to the second-to-last pillar of the Aligned Leadership framework.

Our Contentment

When it comes to embodying our purpose, contentment is a vast and often overlooked piece of the equation. Most of the folks I coach are type A high achievers. I would put myself in that group as well, and maybe you would, too. For those of us who have also come of age in late-stage capitalism, it can feel counterintuitive to prioritize contentment. In fact, contentment isn't part of the work conversation for many of us at all. But contentment is the fuel that lights the way and catalyzes our purpose. If we've arrived at our purpose with contentment in absentia, have we really arrived? (I think by now we should all know the answer to that!) If we wait until we've completed our projects to perfection before we allow ourselves to feel content, then we will wait forever. If we punish ourselves through the process of accomplishing our goals, we forget our why. Being demanding of ourselves and not allowing the ease of contentment usually happens when we're not in the present moment. We're either future tripping or trying to rewrite history. As we evaluate new and existing opportunities, we want to ask ourselves, *Does this support contentment in my life?*

Our Values

Our values inform our behavior, our choices, and what's important to us. When we do work that embodies our values, we feel more aligned with and connected to our purpose. On the other hand, if we work in a place that doesn't uphold the same core principles we do, we can feel crushed by an internal friction. Think about it: Most of us spend more of our heartbeats at work than we do anywhere else. It eclipses time spent with our loved ones, on passion projects, even on hobbies. If we don't share the same core values with our employer, it's going to feel like we're fighting ourselves every day we show up to work. This is why values alignment needs to be one of our criteria. Realistically, some of our values will shift over time because we are evolutionary beings; our needs will change and so might our impact and even the gifts we want to bring forth. Give yourself permission to reevaluate this at every next level of your life.

THE MAJOR UPGRADE

As we wrap up this chapter, I want to invite you into a space of dreaming. Those of us with marginalized identities are often so focused on survival (or chasing a goal someone else outlined for us) that we rarely feel we have permission to step into dreaming. However, if we don't know what our dream is, how can we ever journey toward it?

Let's start by defining what I mean by dream. In the career and personal development world, there is a lot of talk about how "dream jobs" aren't real and the idea of them sets us up to fail. The same goes for "dream partner," "dream home," and everything in between, because everything and everyone in life has its benefits and drawbacks. The dream, in my definition, isn't about perfection—perfection isn't real—but about the major upgrade you want to see in your life. It's about allowing yourself to envision the kind of transformation or elevation you've never let yourself see. It's not a mythic fairy tale—it's a vision for what's next, whether that's better work-life harmony, a specific salary that allows you to travel more, free evenings and weekends for your creative pursuits, or running your own business.

Write down what your major upgrade would be, and as you do, don't worry about how it will come to be. The how often solves itself or shows up when you say yes to yourself. But take this opportunity to give voice to your deepest desires, quite possibly in a way you have never allowed yourself to before.

I also want you to give yourself permission to change your mind. I don't believe in three- or five-year plans because, as we already know, it's better to live directionally, not destinationally. Let one upgrade make way for the next upgrade.

Exercise:
Identify Your Major Upgrade

1. Take a few minutes to write the major upgrade for your work and your life one year from now. Think about how you want to actualize your purpose in an upgraded way. Write it in the present tense and be as descriptive and detailed as you'd like. This is your dream, so please give yourself permission to GO BIG. You can write it as a list or as stream of consciousness, or you can even draw it out—whatever is most clear and supportive for *you*. Think specifically of the areas of your work and life that you want to give a major upgrade to.

2. How is this dream different from your current reality?

3. Are you honoring all five parts of the Aligned Leadership framework? Which parts of the framework do you need to address?

4. What needs to shift in your current reality to fully get on the court with your gifts, values, contentment, needs, and impact?

Now that we're clearer on our purpose and have a method of evaluating possibilities that come our way, you might have a few questions on exactly how to know if something is aligned with your gifts or not. We'll spend the next chapter exploring how you embody your gifts in the deepest and most transformative way. Ready?

Chapter Summary

- Most of us have been taught to be obsessed with our performance, but performance is often an act. Swap performance for purpose.

- Those of us attuned enough to not solely focus on performance often fixate on passion. Too much attention on passion is unsustainable, as it often has us forgo our needs. A career based on passion alone isn't viable for everyone. Those who come from affluent and upper-middle-class backgrounds are better positioned and have the necessary social connections and financial safety nets.

· Toss out the idea of a singular North Star and instead make space for a constellation to express your purpose.

· Living directionally is about following your own inner guidance every step of the way. Give yourself permission to evolve as you go.

· Use the Aligned Leadership framework to evaluate opportunities to ensure they are aligned with who you are.

Chapter 5.

IDENTIFY YOUR TRUE GIFTS

> Every human being is born with a special gift.
> This gift, for each of us, is the doorway to a
> fulfilled life.
>
> —Stephen Cope[1]

A few years ago, I got to work with an amazing woman named Liz. Liz was a journeyman mechanic in Los Angeles, and one of the few women in her field. She was very well liked by her peers and had spent the last nine years really honing her abilities, thus rising to the top with relative ease. But a part of her felt like she was forcing life and work to happen, and as a result, she was miserable. In our first session, she told me story after story about how life in the trades was burning her out and getting her down. But she was at a loss because, as she saw it, this was her gift. How would she pay her bills if she stepped away?

We went through an exercise to help her identify the spectrum of her gifts. One that was readily apparent to both her and me was her emotional intelligence. In fact, within the first three minutes of the call, I was like, *Who is this brilliant, self-aware woman who reads emotions as if she's reading a manual?* When we explored that together, the first thing Liz said was, "Yeah, but isn't everyone like that?" I smiled, because I hear this 90 percent of the time when I'm helping people discover their gifts.

"No way is everyone like that! In fact, few people are," I replied. "This is part of your magic." And as if she'd known it all along but was waiting for permission to acknowledge it for herself, Liz began to cry.

Here's the thing: we all have a unique brilliance within us just waiting to pour forth. Some of us are born knowing what that is and others discover it over time. Part of why many of us find it so difficult to recognize our talents as gifts is because we, like Liz, have a hard time believing that what comes so naturally could ever be perceived as genius. For example, your parents may have only valued careers in finance, so when you demonstrated excellence in journalism, it was dismissed as "not a real career." Thus, we spend an overabundance of time trying to cultivate skills outside of our gifts, forcing us to be good at something our brains weren't made for and that requires a lot of energy. It's precisely that mindset that keeps us fractured in painful ambition.

Unearthing your natural gifts, or genius, is one of the fastest ways to align with purposeful ambition. Unfortunately, as historically excluded people, the world has blurred our vision, making our genius difficult to claim. That's why when I talk about our purpose and our gifts, I refer to the process as an "unearthing," because your gift has been inside you all along, and sometimes we need someone to clean our lenses so we can see it a bit more clearly.

CLAIM YOUR GENIUS WITH THE THREE E'S

Knowing what our natural talents actually are makes it easier to design our work and lives so we make the most meaningful contributions, both for ourselves and others. When helping clients channel their inner genius, the first thing I do is help them identify the areas in which they perform averagely (the eh zone), with proficiency (the excellent zone), and with off-the-charts brilliance (the exceptional zone—or our natural gifts). I call these the Three E's. This framework is inspired by Gay Hendricks's *The Genius Zone*, with a few alterations.

THE THREE E'S

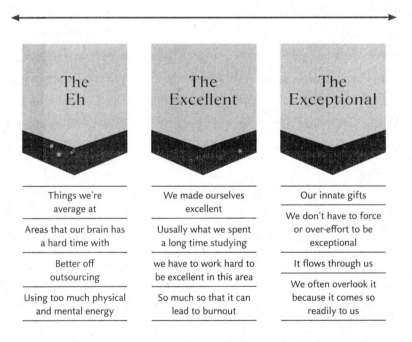

The Eh	The Excellent	The Exceptional
Things we're average at	We made ourselves excellent	Our innate gifts
Areas that our brain has a hard time with	Uusally what we spent a long time studying	We don't have to force or over-effort to be exceptional
Better off outsourcing	we have to work hard to be excellent in this area	It flows through us
Using too much physical and mental energy	So much so that it can lead to burnout	We often overlook it because it comes so readily to us

These three zones are on a continuum because, in reality, we also occupy in-between spaces. We may have some skills that fall between eh and excellent, for example, or between excellent and exceptional. It is virtually impossible to place a complex, multifaceted human into buckets, so allow yourself to also take up the interstitial spaces as well.

The objective of this framework is to help you identify how much time you are spending in each zone so you can begin moving toward operating primarily in your exceptional zone: this is where purposeful ambition thrives. When you work in your exceptional zone, you use much less physical and mental energy, and what you contribute far outpaces what others could. In short, when you apply the best that is within you, what you are capable of expands exponentially. And when you apply the best that is within you, it's not only great for you, it's great for the world. (Remember Jim Rohn's definition of ambition in chapter 1: Ambition is wanting something at the service of others.)

Another benefit of owning your exceptional abilities is that it takes you out of the scarcity mindset. When we believe that genius is reserved for the select few, we fight to compete and be seen. But when we realize we all have unique and exceptional abilities worth sharing, it's clear that there is no competition; we are all in service to one another, and no one is above or below anyone else. What a liberating concept!

Let's explore each of the Three E's in depth, starting with our eh zone and working our way toward the exceptional. And like all the exercises we do in this book, we're doing this through the lens of curiosity and self-compassion, never judgment.

The Eh Zone

The eh zone is comprised of the things we're pretty average at. We can get the job done, but our achievement is by no means excellent or close to exceptional. We perform on par with our peers, maybe even subpar, but it takes a lot of energy and effort to simply be average. This is often one of the easiest zones for us to identify—as soon as we release the egocentric concept that we have to be good at everything, that is. But identifying our eh abilities isn't about judgment. It's about acknowledging the things our brains weren't made for.

Unfortunately, far too many of us spend our days laboring in the eh zone, and then we feel bad about ourselves. For me, some examples of things that fall into my eh zone are admin tasks, website development, and coding—my brain literally does not compute when it comes to these skills. But I used to spend way too much energy on these tasks and not enough on my high-impact areas that brought me meaning, such as coaching. Historically, marginalized people have been forced to spend too much time in our eh zones because we've been told for centuries that we have no genius, which creates a lot of internal dissonance that causes us to underperform. We know we are meant for more, but the structure of the world tries to keep us in a box.

For example, my client Ben, a chief creative officer at a well-known agency, started their career in copy editing. They told me they often felt "stupid" because they would frequently miss minute errors in product copy. But stupidity could not have been further from the truth—they clearly possessed genius but had been working in a space not meant for them. Ben eventually realized they are an incredible visionary and big-picture thinker and can look at a brand and figure out how to revitalize it and tell a story through visuals. They finally admitted that they were "terrible" at copy editing and didn't have the fine attention to detail required to do it. Once they let go of that job and transitioned into design, everything changed—and Ben was much happier in their new role as it finally leveraged their genius.

Now let's use the questions below to help you get clear on your eh abilities. The goal here is to list them and, over time, figure out ways you can shift from these areas so you can focus on using your exceptional gifts to make a greater contribution. We all have different ways of contributing to the world, and it should feel freeing and celebratory to release what isn't for us. It's through that more purposeful contribution that we create a more harmonious relationship with our ambition.

Exercise:
Identify Your Eh Abilities

1. What are you average at that others can do with greater proficiency?

2. What areas does your brain have a hard time understanding and perhaps wasn't designed for?

3. Where do you exert quite a bit of energy and time to produce an average result?

4. Think back to a time where you wasted hours trying to figure something out and still didn't get it. What were you doing?

The Excellent Zone

Unlike in the eh zone, when we're in our zone of excellence, we operate far above average. In fact, we're pretty good at something, and we've probably spent a lot of time refining our skill at that something, perhaps having gone to school or spent the better part of our career developing competency. Yet you find it takes a lot of time and effort, and you have to use up a lot of energy just to reach a certain level. You might even be on the verge of burnout.

The difference between excellence and genius is that while genius is innate, excellence takes a lot out of us. We can be adept at something, yet if that something requires too much of us, it is not our true gift. For example, I would consider writing to be in my zone of excellence. I've spent a long time cultivating my writing skills, from high school English classes to my college thesis to the day-to-day writing I do in my business. But for me to produce excellent work in this space, I need a lot of time and energy. I have to draft and redraft, shaping and chipping away like I'm molding clay. But my editor is exceptional in this area. She has written five of her own books. Her tone shines through everything she writes, from a text message to comments in a Word document. She can look at a piece of writing and tell you where it needs to develop within minutes of reading it. It's her gift.

Unfortunately, most of us spend our lives in our zone of excellence and not our genius because in many ways, it's easier. The pull to stay in the zone of excellence is powerful; it's where your desire for comfort keeps you anchored. Our family, friends, and workplaces prefer us to be in this zone because they benefit tremendously from it as well. In this space, you're dependable, consistently delivering what those around you need in order to be in *their* genius.

If you decide to leave the excellent zone, unfortunately, there will be people who will feel personally affronted by your growth because of the way it impacts them. When I left my marketing career, where I'd excelled but which left me deeply burned out, a lot of people had something to say about it—and it wasn't always favorable. One of the last marketing projects I ever worked on was for a start-up. When I told the founder I was leaving the job—even though I gave months of notice and offered to make the transition as seamless as he needed—he never spoke to me again. My excellence supported his genius. And he was so angry and felt so abandoned, I was tempted to let my genius die rather than to let him down.

The problem with staying in our excellent zone is that it cuts us off from the truest parts of ourselves. In fact, most of my clients come to me when they are doing well but there is a part of them that feels like they're so disconnected from their truth that life feels a bit meaningless. They don't feel fully alive. Moreover, having to work so hard to be excellent at something fosters our painful ambition and hurts us in the long run. Staying in this zone is also what often keeps us in that very competitive place with a strong desire to "win." It fuels competition where there doesn't need to be. We all get to be in our own gifts, making the world better side by side.

Shifting from excellence to genius requires us to come out of our comfort zone, or that psychologically safe space where things are familiar, we feel at ease, and there is low accountability. Leaving is a scary challenge for most of us. But staying doesn't help us grow. Leaving our zone of excellence to embody our exceptional zone means that our desire for growth and change has to be bigger than our fear of leaving behind comfort. It's usually that sacred voice inside ourselves that says it will wither and die if we don't allow it to unfold that gets us to choose the shift—and sometimes it doesn't feel like a choice at all. Sometimes we're thrust into it via being laid off, getting sick, having opportunities dry up, or through some other major redirection.

Let me be clear: I'm not asking you to abandon your excellence, and especially not overnight. It can feel too psychologically unsafe and panic-inducing to do that, because most of us have earned our livings in this zone and can feel like our survival depends on it. Instead, we should move out of our excellent zones gradually.

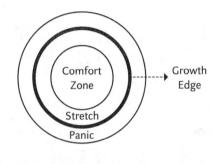

	Psychological Safety	Accountability
Comfort	High	Low
Stretch	High	High
Panic	Low	High

Based on the Zone Model by Karl Rohnke[2]

Use the exercise below to discern your excellent zone. In the next few sections, we're going to identify ways for you to shift more into your exceptional abilities over time.

Exercise:
Identify Your Excellent Abilities

1. What are you really, really good at that you've studied or worked hard for?

2. What do people often compliment you for? (With our excellent abilities, we often receive compliments because these abilities serve other people.)

3. Where have you honed your skills over the years and perhaps clocked your 10,000 hours?

4. What do you contribute that is really excellent, but that also takes a lot out of you to do so?

The Exceptional Zone

When you're in the exceptional zone, you lean into your natural abilities, which are innate. It's easy to get in a flow state. You feel strong, excited, and energized, as if you could continue doing this work nearly indefinitely. You are fully absorbed and utilize not just your skills but the full spectrum of your gifts. There is no one who can do exactly what you are doing in the way you are doing it.

The range of exceptional gifts is as broad as it is unique. Here are some examples of my clients' exceptional abilities—see if you relate to any of these:

- Group facilitation
- Reading the room
- Giving talks
- Selling programs
- Writing and recording guided meditations
- Connecting with people
- Seeing the good in people
- Synthesizing complex ideas

- Writing

- Researching

- Overseeing operations

- Negotiating

- Being the voice of reason

- Marketing

- Leading with empathy

- Diagnosing patients

- Creating intimacy

- Designing nurturing spaces

- Cultivating talent

- Pitching

- Project managing

- Building trust

As you can see, gifts can be a mix of hard skills (specific, learnable skills and abilities we can demonstrate in a measured way) and power skills (formerly known as "soft skills," qualities that support situational awareness and enhance our performance, often synonymous with emotional intelligence). Of course, what might be exceptional for some can be eh for others.

In yoga philosophy it is also believed that the gift is often paired with a wound. As Stephen Cope says:

> They are born together, like twins. This means that many of us must discover our gift in the very heart of our suffering, our difficulty, our struggle. The Eastern contemplative

traditions have a poetic way of saying this: Our gift is like the lotus that is born out of the mud.[3]

If it weren't for my muddy rock-bottom moments, I never would have found my greatest gifts. Years ago, when I was still working in marketing and was looking for a new role, I'd been on about twenty interviews and nothing was aligning. I'd gotten a few offers, but they weren't great. There were a handful of exciting opportunities where I was their second choice, and then there were downright painful experiences that felt humiliating. At the time, I lived just off Thirty-Fourth Street in Manhattan, right along the East River. Every morning, I'd look out hopefully at that sparkling river as I put on my interview suit and headed out to these meetings, praying that one would feel great and I'd get a fantastic offer. And every night, after a strange day of conversations, I'd sit at my window that overlooked the beautiful body of water and cry my eyes out. They were deep heaving sobs of pain and confusion. Salty tears would splash down my blazer as I talked to God and begged for a lifeboat. I had no idea why this moment was so challenging. A part of me felt like I was doing everything wrong. I remember one day, after another disappointing interview, I jokingly said to my friend and roommate, Victoria, "Maybe I was supposed to do this for a living." To somehow make career pivots less awful, I suppose. I had no idea how I would do that—but there is some truth in every joke. My point is, if I hadn't known the deep suffering of that moment, I never would have found my truest and most innate abilities—the ones that have led me here.

Even though these gifts (often born of the mud) are innate, there is sometimes confusion around whether or not we have to work at them. Let me clear that up right now: we must hone our gifts. A child might be born with a natural aptitude for music, but unless they perpetually fine-tune that gift, they will fall short of mastery. I might be a gifted coach, but I never stop there; I continue to better my skills and learn new ones to go deeper in this area.

That said, it is a form of privilege to be able to live in this zone all day, every day. In fact, I don't know anyone who does. Most of us can't go from zero to a hundred overnight because our workplaces and the structure of our lives simply don't allow for that. The goal is to move as close to your exceptional abilities as you can each day so you can live in greater satisfaction and fulfillment. One way to do this, as Gay Hendricks suggests in *The Big Leap*, is by spending ten uninterrupted minutes a day in our genius. This can look like journaling or starting a painting practice, or even offering ten-minute mini sessions with your gift. After that becomes routine for you, move up to fifteen minutes. Eventually, over time, the balance can shift, and we can spend most of our days doing what we do best. As you spend more time in your genius, you may want to consider shifting your role or transitioning to something new. As I mentioned before, it doesn't always feel psychologically safe to do that overnight. So perhaps you start with some volunteer work in that zone. Once you build confidence then maybe you launch a side gig. And with each extra minute, you become stronger and stronger, eventually getting to spend a great many of your heartbeats in that area.

As you think about releasing what doesn't serve you and others and embodying what does, I want you to think deeply about how your family, community, and the world will shift as a result. This isn't just for you (though that is reason enough). This is for everyone who has been stifled or had to hide who they really are.

What if Serena Williams had never used her genius on the tennis court?

What if Betty White had never expressed her gift of comedy?

What if Beyoncé had never grabbed the mic to sing her way into our hearts and souls?

What if Mister Rogers had never shared his passion for connecting with children?

We'd live in a very different world, my friends. Your liberated ambition gives permission for others to be liberated, too.

Exercise:
Identify Your Exceptional Abilities

1. When do you feel most alive and energized? What are you doing or sharing? How are you showing up? How are you feeling?

2. When do you find yourself in the space of flow? When do you fully lose track of time because you are so immersed and wonderfully carried away in the waves of that thing?

3. When you join a work or social group, what do you uniquely contribute that wasn't there before?

4. What do people seek you out for most often?

5. Where are the moments that you've surprised yourself in your ability to rise to a new height or solve a unique and difficult challenge with ease and grace?

6. If you're unsure, ask two to five friends who really see you what they think your gifts are. (The key here is friends who really see you. Often when we ask others, they project onto us, so I believe it's always a good measure to look inward first.)

IDENTIFYING YOUR HIGHEST-YIELD GIFTS

By this point, hopefully you have a better sense of your exceptional gifts and those that aren't quite in that zone. This information can help point you toward the expression of your purpose and inform how you want to be spending your time here on earth so you can feel more whole. Next, we're going to categorize them into what we like to do and don't like to do. After all, just because we're *good* at something doesn't mean we *like* to do it. The ones we're exceptional at and enjoy are your highest-yield contribution and where you can make the biggest difference. With these insights, we can redesign our days and weeks so they can better utilize our genius.

Using the lines in the graphic, separate your abilities into the ones you enjoy doing and the ones you do not. It's helpful to list them out across all three zones at once so you can see the big picture.

	EH	EXCELLENT	EXCEPTIONAL
LIKE 👍	_____	_____	_____
	_____	_____	_____
	_____	_____	_____
	_____	_____	_____
DISLIKE 👎	_____	_____	_____
	_____	_____	_____
	_____	_____	_____
	_____	_____	_____

Now that we know where our genius is and where it isn't, we want to design our work around our most impactful gifts. And sometimes that can feel impossible—I've been there! The objective is to start small and continue to build each and every day. Let's say you are the VP of sales at a large organization and your most exceptional ability is connecting with people. But through this exercise you became aware that you spend most of your time in your excellent ability of strategic planning. I would invite you to jot down a few ways you could spend more time connecting with people while simultaneously identifying how you might coach someone on your team to take on more of the strategic planning. Then I'd suggest you open your calendar and schedule ten minutes a day for the next few weeks to connect with people.

Exercise:
Move Closer to Your Exceptional Abilities

1. When you look at a calendar of your week, where or on what do you currently spend most of your time? Are these items inside your exceptional abilities or excellent abilities?

2. What is the biggest thing that zaps your time and energy and keeps you outside of your exceptional or excellent abilities?

3. What are some items on your list that fall into your eh zone, or that you don't like doing, that you could resource in another way?

4. Pick three of your exceptional abilities that you want to turn the volume up on. What is your plan to go deeper with those gifts in the next ninety days? How can you start with just ten minutes a day and move up from there?

STACK YOUR GENIUS

When I invite clients to identify and own their genius, they will often say, "But so many other people can lead/synthesize ideas/play the cello/do this thing. Is my gift really special?" First of all, it *is* really special. But second, your innate gift becomes even richer and more far-reaching when you combine, or stack, it with your other gifts.

My client Reema is a perfect example of a genius-stacker in action. She is a registered-nurse-turned-interior-design-virtuoso. One of her exceptional abilities is creating nurturing spaces; she was able to do this both as a healthcare professional and when she transitioned to her interior design practice. But she didn't stop there—and this is where the magic happens. Reema also had *energetic* gifts. She was attuned with reiki, astrology, and feng shui, and she brought together these gifts into an offering she called the Jupiter Method.

The Jupiter Method was unlike anything anyone had ever heard of. Reema would read your astrology chart along with your family's, then leverage feng shui and the art of interior design to create spaces that were literally arranged to serve your highest potential. Bringing together all of her forms of genius allowed her to create a completely new and exciting offering that served people in a way that nothing else had or could. Stacking our genius changes the game because there's no competition when we are fully ourselves.

When it comes to stacking your genius, I want you to think beyond tangible skills to the vehicle and context. Maybe you are an exceptional astrologer and have always given phone readings.

Great, but a lot of people do that. Perhaps another one of your gifts is creating experiential events that help people transform, and a third gift is storytelling. Genius-stacking these gifts could look like creating a series of immersive experiences, designed around astrological events, that tell the story of the time we're in. See how things just got a lot more interesting and textured? When we put all the wonderful parts of us together, we create more dimension.

When genius-stacking, it's also helpful to leverage your lived experience. I shared earlier that our gift is often paired with a wound, and we can use our challenges to help uncover our gifts. If I hadn't gotten sick, for example, I likely wouldn't have created a curriculum that really honors people's bodies, hearts, minds, and careers. Think about how your unique lived experience has taught you certain lessons that might not be ubiquitous, and how you can combine those lessons with your genius to create something game-changing. There are likely tools and methods you're combining in your own life already. A life full of purposeful ambition is one where we let all of our genius speak.

Exercise:
Genius-Stack Your Life

1. What are your forms of genius that you love sharing and expressing the most?

2. How can you bring together those forms of genius to create something that is a unique expression of you?

3. What has your lived experience taught you that others might not know yet? How can you combine that with your genius?

4. What are things that other people aren't putting together that you're naturally combining in your own life?

5. What unique vehicles or contexts can you create to bring your genius together in an ownable way?

DEMOCRATIZING GENIUS

Unfortunately, not everyone feels permission to own their genius, because for millennia we've been sold a story about who gets to be a genius and who doesn't. For instance, in a 2018 Pew Research study, participants deemed the words *powerful, leadership,* and *ambition* to be more positive in men than in women, while the words *compassionate* and *caring* were considered positive traits for women but negative ones for men.[4] And an analysis of reviews on RateMyProfessor.com found that Black professors and female professors were less likely to be considered "genius" than their white male peers.[5] No wonder we abandon some of our gifts—we as a society are told that certain attributes only matter when embodied by the "right" person, aka white and male. As a result, many of us experience a complete lack of connection and belonging around work, and we question our right to take up space. We struggle to have the confidence we need to be our genius selves—and it can feel like swimming upstream. (Which, again, leads to the ambition trap.)

It doesn't just happen on an individual basis—we see it happening in our cultures. Let's take Zaha Hadid, the late, famed Iraqi architect known as the "queen of the curve" because of her futuristic designs (which for a long time were called unbuildable because engineers couldn't keep pace with her vision). In 2004, Hadid became the *first* woman to ever receive the coveted Pritzker Architecture Prize, an award given to living architects who have made considerable contributions and achievements in the field. Since Hadid's win, five other female architects have received this most notable accolade. Yet the press covering Hadid's win was less than celebratory. The media labeled her a "diva," even publicly psychoanalyzing her temperament. A *New York Times* article on her read, "Ms. Hadid has only recently found the clients willing to look beyond her reputation for being difficult."[6] Like much of the rhetoric we see around ambitious women of color, she was built up and taken down all in the same breath.

Even the way we define genius is laced with bias. A few years back, I was leading a workshop and talking about how "genius," "brilliance," and "gifts" are synonymous (which is why you'll find them used interchangeably in this book) when a participant's hand shot up. She said, "But genius is different, because it's quantifiably measured." This is what most of us have been led to believe—it's what IQ tests are for, right? But IQ metrics, and standardized testing in general, all hinge on the idea that our brilliance is an objective numerical variable. Moreover, being seen as brilliant by our teachers depends on educators being unbiased when dealing with students across race and cultures. (Unfortunately, the data suggests this is often not the case, with teachers showing greater implicit bias toward students of color.[7]) What we do know is that more than intelligence, IQ tests actually measure how motivated students are during testing.[8] Therefore, there is no universal standard of measure for our genius.

Unfortunately, it's not just those with dominant identities who perpetuate the message that genius is for the select few. Under the patriarchy, even women have come to believe this. In a 2015 study on contradictory attitudes, 87 percent of female participants answered that geniuses tend to be male.[9] Other studies have shown that "girls' own-gender brilliance perceptions were lower than boys'."[10] And these ideas have been long in the making. In fact, since the time of the Greeks, genius has traditionally been defined as male, with roots tracing back to ancient Rome. Literature and history books tell us that genius can be all sorts of men, but according to Christine Battersby, author of *Gender and Genius*, it's always a "'Hero,' and never a heroine."[11]

What all of this does is create a sense of scarcity around genius in which we believe only a few can wield it, and so we work more and more to prove ourselves worthy. This kind of approach has far-reaching repercussions across our culture of work, however, including giving rise to the "toxic visionary." The toxic visionary is a leader so revered for their genius, we let their harmful and often dehumanizing treatment of others slide.

For example, when I was first writing this book, the news cycle was covering the infamous FTX scandal. FTX, formerly one of the world's largest cryptocurrency exchanges, was founded by a man named Sam Bankman-Fried. Bankman-Fried was hailed as the "boy wonder of crypto," as he established one of the biggest cryptocurrency exchanges in the world and gained wealth faster than nearly anyone in history.[12] It was reported that in a pitch meeting with a venture capital firm, Bankman-Fried was caught rudely playing *League of Legends*—but the group was purportedly so impressed with him and his irreverence, that they went on to fund his venture.[13] Would you ever, in a million years, imagine a woman or person of color getting away with the same impertinence? Eventually, Bankman-Fried was arrested for fraud. His company had built its business on risky trading options that are not legal in the United States, and while it was once a $32 billion global empire, FTX eventually imploded and filed for bankruptcy.

The toxic visionary traits endorsed by powerful organizations only makes a healthy relationship to ambition more challenging for the rest of us. If we honor the truth that all of us have genius, those abusing this power lose the ability to use it to cover such offenses. This is why unearthing our gifts is one of the fastest ways to align with purposeful ambition. When we democratize genius by reminding ourselves that we all have some, we shatter the myth of hierarchy. Some of us were raised with the belief that to embody a certain gift made them better than others. In some families, to be great at math is better than being great at writing. Or being a teacher is better than being a business owner. None of these ideas are universally true. To have any gift is a magical thing. And when we each remember our own, we're not fighting to compete and be the best based on someone else's arbitrary measure. We are basking in the glory of our own contribution and its interdependence with other people's. That is what it means for all of us to be in purposeful ambition together. There is no competition when we each occupy all the corners, edges, and pockets of our own true gifts.

THE CONFIDENCE YOU NEED

Owning and living into our genius requires a certain level of confidence. You may be an exceptional writer but starting a Substack probably feels terrifying because you're opening yourself up to criticism by sharing your work in such a public way (not to mention you might not know how to make money with it immediately). It may also mean letting people down by giving up your day job to bet on yourself and start the business you've always wanted to. Thankfully, spending time in our genius also builds our confidence. Just like at the gym, with every repetition we get stronger.

So how do we build enough confidence to seize our exceptional abilities? I love author, educator, and activist Brittany Packnett Cunningham's advice. According to her, confidence requires three things: *permission, community,* and *curiosity*. Confidence requires that we give it permission to exist. Community is the safest place for us to nurture that confidence. And curiosity sustains it by inviting us to keep learning and exploring.[14]

I couldn't agree more. If we try on confidence in spaces where we don't have permission to, we will stop before we even get started. But if we explore our Three E's in community and through the lens of curiosity, we give ourselves room to learn and play and try things on, like we did as children. For example, when my clients are trying on their exceptional abilities for size, I invite them to share those gifts in safe community spaces. You might have a group of friends you can practice your new yoga teachings with. Or perhaps you can give a talk to your meditation community before pitching that talk to a TED stage. Or like me, you can volunteer to coach old teammates who know, like, and trust you so you feel safe to receive feedback. Where are your little pockets of community and how can you tap into them to practice your gifts?

⚘

Our confidence, our contributions, and our ambition become more far-reaching when we live into all our gifts. Claiming and owning that you have many exceptional abilities allows you to work from a place of your fullest expression and therefore make the greatest impact. Life becomes a place of boundless possibility. But being sustained in that impact means we have to honor our needs, and we're about to do a big deep dive on that.

Chapter Summary

———◇———

- We all have exceptional abilities just waiting to pour forth from us. The idea that genius is for the select few or is a singular numerical value is a patriarchal myth.

- Accept what comes most naturally to you. I know we want to discount those areas—but that's your magic.

- Use the Three E's to find your eh, excellent, and exceptional abilities, then design your work around your gifts. Start with just an extra ten minutes a day in your gifts and see what happens.

- Transitioning into more of your genius requires psychological safety and confidence. It's often not an overnight shift, though it can be. Build that confidence in community.

- Stack the different forms of your genius to create the most unique expression.

Chapter 6.

MEET YOUR NEEDS

You don't have to earn the right to have a need.

—KATE NORTHRUP[1]

We cannot get into a right relationship with our ambition, nor live out our purpose, if our needs aren't being met. For most of us, especially those of us who have been historically excluded, honoring our needs can feel like a foreign concept. We've been taught that everyone gets to go before we do, that our needs are the least important. But as the old adage goes, you cannot pour from an empty cup. And even if you're not currently pouring, you never have to earn the right to have your needs met. You deserve to have your cup filled.

My client Rayyan learned this the hard way. He worked in HR for one of the world's largest media companies and was responsible for ensuring their employee resources groups received appropriate funding and support for their initiatives. As a neurodivergent person of color and immigrant, he found this work deeply meaningful. However, the major emotional demands of the role soon started to take a toll.

What Rayyan realized early on was that not all resource groups were receiving equal funding, further perpetuating inequities within the company. Person after person would come to him to vent, seeking emotional support. He felt stuck between a rock and a hard place: he was advocating for these groups but was not able to get them what they needed, then had to deal with the fallout. Plus, he started doing crisis work inside the organization. Between everything, he was pulling twelve-plus-hour workdays, while also being a dad to two young children.

When Rayyan came to me, he was feeling very low and was about to take a leave of absence to support his mental health. And while we did talk about how he might shift his role, the deeper question became, what was getting in the way of him properly taking care of himself? Because after a ten-minute conversation, it became clear to me that Rayyan had not been doing that. He had stopped writing, which he loved so much. He rarely made time for yoga, which had been his go-to movement practice. On top of everything, he felt guilty about needing to take time off and the burden it would place on his partner.

As the classic saying goes, we are human beings, not human doings. We are not designed to be in perpetual motion. We need time, energy, and resources to be able to pace and replenish ourselves. As one of my teachers, Rha Goddess, says, "Self-sacrifice is not a contribution." In fact, it's often a hallmark of codependency—and a surefire bet for burnout.

Unfortunately, many of us don't feel like we have permission to take care of ourselves, or we don't know how. The first step is to figure out where our resentment line lies.

LIVING ABOVE THE RESENTMENT LINE

I first heard about the resentment line from fellow coach Danielle Cohen. Most of us have an imaginary line in our minds that, when crossed, makes us resentful. For some of us it's when our clients pay too little yet ask too much. For others, it's when the work takes us away from our families more than we'd like. We get in trouble because many of us haven't told people where our resentment line lies—thus they trespass over it all day every day, making us bitter, angry, and exhausted. But we're not able to let others know where the line is if we don't know for ourselves.

When it comes to honoring our needs, we need to be clear on where our resentment line resides. If we don't know where that line is for ourselves, we will spend our lives in painful ambition, overworking our bodies and letting fear and anger lead. From the mother who gives too much of herself to her children, to the service provider who charges her clients too little, to the manager who spends way too many hours coaching their direct reports and not enough developing their own skills, we need to be intimately acquainted with where this line is.

For example, when my brilliant client Nora, a pharmaceuticals exec, first started her own business after working for prestigious yet toxic companies across the country, she lived way below the resentment line. She enlisted me to help. When we first explored what she offered and her pricing, I noticed Nora wanted to start with a relatively low retainer compared to the value of the package and her experience. After coaching her through this for a bit, we decided she would start there to get her first client and the next month she would raise the prices to be more commensurate with the offer's value. But when the next month rolled around, she kept her low-priced offer.

Soon she was flooded with work but not flooded with funds. As she couldn't yet afford to hire help, she was doing everything herself. Nora was now working around the clock, not taking breaks, and starting to feel particularly embittered. She hopped on a coaching call, looking defeated and drained. When I asked her what was up, Nora shared how annoyed she was with her clients. They were asking for so much, she said, and their expectations were greatly imbalanced. I revisited the question I had asked her when she first designed her offer: "Nora, did you price this below the resentment line?"

Until this moment, the resentment line had merely been a construct to Nora. But after a few months of working this way, she was not loving her life. Together we redesigned her fees to support her living above that tricky little line. With that one shift, she could now hire help and afford to take weekends off to be with her son.

Oftentimes we operate below the resentment line—doing extra work, not charging enough, or going beyond our capacity—because we want to please people or not make them mad, or because we feel like we should be doing people a favor. But living down there serves no one. If you show up to work in a perpetually bad mood, feeling aggrieved by the weight of what you reluctantly agreed to, everyone will feel it and no one will actually benefit—especially you. Everyone wins when we live above the resentment line.

So how do we make sure we're living above that thorny line?

- Get clear on your capacity: Identify how many hours a week you can work or how many clients you can take on before you start to feel resentful. Knowing how much you can work will also inform your pricing. We want to cultivate agility around our capacity, as certain seasons will ask more of us and certain seasons will ask less.

- Set boundaries: Get clear on what you're willing to do, what you won't do, and what you will make exceptions for. Perhaps you're not willing to take calls on the weekend but will make exceptions for emergencies.

- Know your trade-offs: When our plate is already full and we say yes to something new, it means we'll have to say no to something else. Know what your trade-offs are and communicate them outward. For example, if you say yes to a promotion and more responsibility, maybe you need to say no to doing your own admin.

- Ensure you're resourced: Resourced people can resource others. Ensure you're paid appropriately, get enough sleep, and are nourishing yourself in supportive ways. That way you can extend energy outward and still have enough for yourself. More on this next!

PRIORITIZE YOUR WELL-BEING

Living above the resentment line means making the space and time to nourish ourselves, not just when we're depleted but long before we get to that point. It's nearly impossible to show up as our whole beings if we aren't continuously taking care of ourselves in supportive ways and in the areas that are important to us. And I don't just mean the food we eat and the way we move our bodies (if we have that privilege), but also the people we surround ourselves with, our relationship to our finances, and so much more that encompasses self-care. According to Sarah Tacy Tangredi, a mind/body trainer to former Olympians, executives, and leaders, our nervous systems thrive when we have "greater resources than demands." Nourishing ourselves is a way to make sure we have the resources we need for the demands that might be coming our way. It allows us to get ahead of burnout and depletion, and to get more swiftly to the place where we operate optimally: to *thriving*.

However, we cannot talk about nourishment without acknowledging the classist aspects of self-care. The modern self-care industry we see so widely on social media often has a capitalistic component, heralding $150 moisturizers, designer leggings, and sound baths with healers as prerequisites for wellness (candidly, I have paid for all of these things in my search for peace). But historically excluded people tend to have less access to rest, often have to work more, and are statistically earning less money on average—making self-care, in the way social media portrays it, accessible to only the select few.

But self-care, especially for marginalized groups, was never about what we can buy—it was about what contributes to our self-preservation and dignity. It's not caring for ourselves if we run up credit card debt to purchase the highly touted lotions and classes that don't address our inner needs. Caring for ourselves starts on the inside, and it happens on both an individual and community level. Self-care is meant to intersect with community care. And because Black, brown, queer, and disabled bodies are consistently valued below cis, white, abled bodies, caring for ourselves in this way is a radical act. The self-care we see portrayed on social media (because it's externally focused) fuels painful ambition, while real self-care (because it's internally oriented and collective) fuels our purposeful ambition.

Self-care is arguably even more important for us because our lived experiences often have more headwinds than tailwinds, which creates a knock-on effect for our health. My dad was a cardiovas-cular surgeon, and I remember him telling me that a lot of his pa-tients who were people of color and immigrants had heart disease (himself included), which he believed was the inevitable outcome of decades of racism and xenophobia that they faced in the US. Turns out, he wasn't wrong. The Centers for Disease Control and the American Medical Association classify discrimination as a health risk.[2] Experiencing bias is associated with elevated cardiovascular disease risk among African immigrants.[3] We need real self- and community care to be able to shift some of these dynamics and thrive.

Let's look at the two steps we can take to strengthen our rela-tionship to self-care, together.

Step One: Gauge the Ways You're Nourishing Yourself (and the Ways You Are Not)

Most of us have not had our needs met consistently, and this can cause a needs deficit that impacts our relationships and how we move through the world, where we end up chasing those unmet needs outside of ourselves through partnerships or work opportu-nities. Sounds a lot like painful ambition, right?

Oftentimes when we're not nurturing ourselves in the spaces and ways we need, it's because there is a story there. Perhaps it's a societally induced story, or a belief from your lineage, or one you created yourself. Maybe you're not taking care of your finances be-cause you believe someone is supposed to swoop in and save you. Or perhaps you're not eating in a way that's supportive to your body because you feel your body needs to be a certain size to be worthy. We want to get a sense of what is intercepting your ability to care for yourself and honor your needs so we can shift it. Only from that place of nourishment can we be more present in our relationship to ambition, because if you finally get the job you want but you get there sick and with zero time for yourself, it's not going to feel so good.

When working with clients, I have them use my nourishment meter to assess the areas in which they are giving themselves the resources they need, and the areas in which they could use a little bolstering. There are thirteen areas we look at:

1. Time
2. Food
3. Community
4. Emotional health
5. Money
6. Movement
7. Spirituality
8. Relationship to self
9. Play
10. Work
11. Boundaries
12. Love life
13. Sex life

Try it out for yourself in the following exercise. Be sure to select the areas that pertain to you and discard the ones that don't. For example, if you are asexual, your sex life is not an important source of nourishment for you, so you can discard that. If you do not have the privilege of moving your body, I would discard movement. If there's an area that makes sense for your life but is not currently listed, add it in.

Exercise:
Complete the Nourishment Meter

NOURISHMENT METER

1   2   3   4   5   6   7   8   9   10

Time
Do you have plenty of time, or do you constantly feel the pressure of it?

Food
Do you have a healthy relationship with food, or is there room for improvement?

Community
Do you have a communities that supports you in different areas of your life?

Emotional Health
Do you feel balanced and supported in your emotional well-being?

Money
Do you feel abundant or tight in the space of money?

Movement
Do you have a movement practice that feels nourishing to you, such as regular workouts, walks, or stretching?

Spirituality
Do you have a spiritual practice that allows you to feel more connected?

Relationship to Self
How nourishing and supportive is your relationship to self? Do you have a healthy inner dialogue?

Play
How much play and levity do you have in your life?

Work
Does work fill up your cup or is it a detractor?

Boundaries
Do you have healthy boundaries or are they wishy-washy?

Love Life
How nourishing does your love life feel?

Sex Life
Do you feel fed by your sex life?

1. For each area of the nourishment meter that feels important to you, answer the following question: How whole, full, and nourished do I feel in this area on a scale of 1–10, with 10 being the most nourished?

2. Focus on the area where you feel the least nourished or fulfilled. What's happening in this space? What is the voice of fear or doubt saying? Is there a story there? I like to look at any area that you've rated a 6 or lower.

3. What's getting between you and feeling most nourished in this area? Sometimes this can require a mindset shift. If so, please revisit chapter 2 on limiting beliefs.

4. What do you need to do in order to fill yourself up more fully in this area?

5. What do you need to not do to fill yourself up more fully in this area? This question might be tricky, but an example might be: to feel more nourished in my boundaries, I need to say no to things I feel like I have to say yes to.

6. Now make a list of what you need to do before work, during work, and after work to stay nourished in these areas.

7. Who will hold you accountable?

Step Two: Identify Your Must-Haves, Nice-to-Haves, and Deal-Breakers

At the basic level, we all need food, shelter, and clothing. But beyond that, we have different requirements that, when fulfilled, allow us to show up more fully. For example, you may live in an expensive metropolitan area and therefore require a high salary to prosper. Or if you are a macro-level visionary, you may need a team to help you bring micro ideas to fruition. Or if you find yourself to be more introverted, you may want more time alone to regulate and recover. When you identify what is important to you and intentionally go out of your way to meet those needs, you cannot help but show up and shine.

Let's get real and clear about your unique requirements. For each aspect of the nourishment meter that pertains to you, make a must-have, nice-to-have, and deal-breaker list.

Let's take work, for example. A must-have for me is mutual respect with people I work with. Getting to work together in person is fun and nourishing but it's a nice-to-have. A deal-breaker is being asked to do anything that would compromise my values—like collaborating with a company that isn't committed to an equitable work environment.

This is one of the simplest but most clarifying exercises I do with my clients. It's especially supportive because so many of us who are historically excluded are so used to moving through the world without having our needs met—from safety and belonging to self-esteem—that we often don't know what we're missing. My client Amber, for example, was a hardworking single mother of two. She worked in resource allocation helping to staff internal teams for projects. Though she was amazing at her job and very well respected, she was grossly underpaid and under-supported.

HONORING OUR NEEDS

Area of the Nourishment Meter we're focused on: _____

Must-Haves:	Nice-to-Haves:	Deal-Breakers:
• •	• •	• •

When we made the list of her must-haves for work, here's what she put:

- $150,000 salary

- Administrative support

- A forty-hour workweek

- No weekend or overtime work except in emergency situations

- Clarity around her role (an actual job description)

- Empowerment to make her own decisions

- A sense of belonging

- Work that leverages her genius

This isn't a lot to ask for, but Amber had gone so long without these things that she wasn't even sure she could get them. But having these resources meant she could show up as her highest and best self and contribute in the way she wanted to.

You deserve to have your needs met. We all do. When our needs are tended to and we're not driven by an aching wound, our relationship to ambition, how we strive and what we strive for, becomes much more intentional.

PRACTICE COMMUNITY CARE

Self-care alone isn't enough, because none of us exists in a vacuum. Our well-being is an extension of the well-being of the communities we belong to. So to really flourish, we need community care.

Community care is the practice of supporting both ourselves and our wider community at the same time, and it has existed in both BIPOC and QTBIPOC spaces for generations. The goal of community care is for those with power, privilege, and resources to support those who are in and around their communities. An essential aspect of community care is recognizing the inequities that exist and are often tied to systemic barriers like economic circumstances, lack of access to quality healthcare, and our physical environments, which directly impact individuals' well-being. To shift these barriers, we must collectively increase access to meaningful resources that affect everyone in the community, and not just take care of ourselves as individuals.

The challenge with this is that in the US, we often prioritize individualism over togetherness. According to activist, educator, and writer Dr. Tema Okun, this cultural attachment "leads to a toxic denial of our essential interdependence and the reality that we are all in this, literally, together."[4] But denying interconnectedness is something only those more dominant in a society can afford to do. Individualism means success is solely based on personal effort, which overlooks the impact of social factors like race, class, and gender. Therefore, individualism upholds and perpetuates unequal power dynamics.

The truth is, we achieve nothing on our own. Even our self-care practices are supported by others, from the metta meditation taught to you by your Buddhist teacher, to the artisan who made your bath salts, to the yogi who offered you the journaling prompts. There is nothing wrong with being interconnected. We humans are social beings. We need one another to survive.

To engage in community care, there are a few things we might do:

- Identify your communities: This may sound completely obvious, but many of us have spent so much time alone or buying into the myth of individualism that we feel disconnected from our communities. Your community can be your family of origin or other chosen family. It can be the community connected to your faith, like your church, mosque, or temple. Community spaces can also be cultural centers connected to our countries of origin, or even our gym, coworking space, meditation center, or library.

- Ask for help: If you're navigating a challenging moment, make it known to your community that you need resources to thrive, whether that's transportation to and from doctors' appointments, help with meals, administrative support, therapy, or even assistance in getting personal care items. Making the ask can feel really vulnerable, but as I mentioned in the previous chapter, community is the safest place to try new things. So practice asking for help if you need it.

- Make it known you're available to help: Much of the time, we're afraid to ask people for help because most of us already have pretty full plates. Let your community know what you're available to contribute. Perhaps it's a ride to the grocery store, participating in a weekly free healing circle, or simply sitting with folks and providing company. Get clear on the ways you uniquely can and would be happy to contribute, and make sure it's clear to your community. You can even create a shared spreadsheet with your community members and what you are each willing to provide.

GET THE MONEY YOU NEED (AND WANT)

A big part of honoring our needs, especially as historically excluded people, rests on making enough money to do so. In this section, I want to explore how to build a healthier relationship to money so it doesn't fuel a harmful relationship with ambition.

The first step is to acknowledge that the playing field has never been equal. There have long been significant inequities in income for historically excluded people, from the racial and gender pay gaps to the vast disparities faced by queer and trans folks. To really contextualize this, let's look at some of the data for those of different identities (though I want to emphasize that, of course, we are not monoliths; this research is just meant to highlight what I have found is true for a lot of us):

- On average, women earn eighty-three cents on a man's dollar.[5]

- Just 6 percent of women will make six figures or more compared with 13 percent of men.[6]

- Only 2 percent of women-owned businesses will make it to seven figures.[7]

- Women-led start-ups receive less than 3 percent of VC funding.[8]

- On average, LGBTQ+ workers earn ninety cents on the dollar earned by a "typical worker."[9]

- LGBTQ+ people who graduated with bachelor's degrees reported that their earnings are 22 percent lower ten years after graduation, compared with cis-het graduates.[10]

- The poverty rate for transgender men was 33.7 percent, for transgender women 29.6 percent, and for gender-nonconforming people 23.8 percent; in comparison, the rate for cisgender heterosexual men was 13.4 percent, and for cisgender heterosexual women it was 17.8 percent.[11]

- The median salary in the US for a person with a disability is $46,887, while the median salary for those without a disability is $55,208.[12]

- Almost 26 percent of people with a disability in the United States were living in poverty compared with 11.5 percent of people without disabilities.[13]

- The Black poverty rate is more than double the white poverty rate in the US.[14]

- White households held 84 percent of wealth in the US (despite being 60 percent of the population), while Black families held just 4 percent of wealth (despite being 13.4 percent of the population).[15]

At first, these stats may be discouraging. A lot of us who live out this financial inequality every single day start to believe it is our fate never to make what we need because of who we are. Many of us don't feel worthy of earning more because we haven't always seen people like us making large amounts of money or enjoying positions of power. Or you might be like the old me, who made a lot of money but gave it all away because I didn't think I deserved it. However, in order to get the money we need and deserve to thrive, we have to reshape our beliefs around what is possible for us as well.

My client Chiara has firsthand experience with this. Chiara is a talented Silicon Valley software engineer who spent her career working for Fortune 100 companies. In her early twenties she had been involved in a cycling accident that caused a traumatic brain injury that eventually resulted in chronic fatigue syndrome. When she disclosed her condition to her manager in her first role, they clapped back with "Good luck finding a place willing to accommodate you!" Immediately Chiara felt a deep sense of shame that she began to carry everywhere. To compensate for this, she even went on to get several advanced degrees to showcase her value. From that day on, she felt so apologetic of her condition, she would never ask for a signing bonus, negotiate her pay, or ask for raises. She just felt lucky to even have a job. She was always worried about rocking the boat and would accept whatever came her way—even abusive and fickle contract positions. So unstable was her career that, at one point, she lost her apartment.

When Chiara came to work with me, she was on the tail end of another abusive and underpaid position, and she desperately wanted stability and humanity in her next role. Much of the work we did together was around releasing the deep shame that had been planted into her brain as a result of her harmful manager reinforcing the bias that people with disabilities don't deserve to be supported. Together, we mapped out what she needed and *how much* she needed to actually thrive in her life. It became abundantly clear that if she wanted to take care of her health and honor her worth, Chiara could no longer accept the crumbs that corporate America was giving her. We identified the must-haves for her next role, and she ultimately landed an eminent VP of engineering position at a Fortune 50 company that was grateful to have her. She got the good insurance, was able to go back to therapy, and caught up on her health and dental care, which she had had to put off for years.

Yes, it has been the rule that most marginalized communities have consistently earned less and have had less access to resources—however, there have also been exceptions. Reminding ourselves of the exceptions from a belief perspective, while also doing the work in our communities and lobbying for systemic change, is where we start to see a shift in our relationship to ambition. There is so much injustice when it comes to earning, lending, and even education around money. *And* we can achieve wealth in our lives for us and those who identify the same way we do.

When we rob people of the ability to earn well, we take away their ability to live. It can truly be a death sentence. We can't even enter the conversation of purposeful ambition if we're always living in survival mode.

When historically excluded people have more, we do more good. For example, when women have more money, they invest 90 percent of it into their families, while when men have more money, they invest 44 percent.[16] Let's talk about how you can get the money you desire so you can honor your needs and be a part of that change.

Heal the Core Wounds and Rewrite Your Story

If your desire for more money is coming from a place of rejection, abandonment, injustice, betrayal, or humiliation (the core wounds we explored in chapter 1), it's going to create a wobbly foundation for your relationship with your finances. Let's say you felt abandoned as a child. Your parents perpetually chose work and their friends over you. When you started your career you thought, *If I can just make enough money for them to see what a shining star I am, they'll love me that way I needed to be loved and all will be well!* Unfortunately, it *rarely* happens that way. Usually, the originators of our core wounds will continue their patterns, not because they're bad people, but because they are unknowingly acting them out or because they haven't done the actual work it takes to heal. Then we toil away for years to reconcile this wound, getting more but feeling emptier still.

Focusing on mindset alone when it comes to money isn't enough—especially for underrecognized people, because it doesn't account for the impact of trauma, oppression, and systemic factors beyond the individual. However, mindset *is* a part of it. We need to look at the mindsets and stories that originated in tandem with our core wounds.

Earlier in the book we explored your mindset and core limiting beliefs—or beliefs that keep us stuck. We hold those same types of ideas about money, whether we realize it or not. I have an exercise below to help you find some of your money stories.

Connect Your Money to Your Why—
and Ground It in Reality

When we yearn for a certain amount of money, and that yearning comes from a place of pain versus a place of purpose, our appetite is insatiable. We'll stop at nothing—even our own well-being—to get what we want. Connecting our aspirations for more money to our why, our mission, and our purpose is more sustainable. We stop fighting the world because we feel like it owes us something and instead become convinced that more money will help us do more good and support more of our why.

Connecting our money to our purpose also helps us go the distance. When the going gets tough, we remember the faces of our children, who we're doing this for. Or we think of our parents, who we're working to help retire. Or we march onward thinking of all the others we're going to inspire. It shifts the aspiration from the head to the heart, a much more generative place to be working from.

Once we've connected our desire for more to our purpose, we also want to be sure to ground it in reality. What I mean by that is, think about how you would use, save, or direct that money so you're clear on its role in your life. Oftentimes we have trouble asking for a certain amount because it feels disconnected from our everyday. We might think, *Do I really need to ask for that much? What will I even do with it?* This is why it's better to figure it out beforehand. A coach once said to me, "Doing the math grounds our nervous system." I know that to be true for myself and my clients. Break down how you would spend, save, and invest your additional money in service to your purpose.

Negotiate for Yourself and Your Community

Negotiating an offer not only helps ensure you receive a salary that accurately reflects your skills, experience, and the value you bring, but expands the bands for everyone who identifies as you do. This is particularly important for historically excluded groups, who may get lower initial offers. Through negotiation—and not just salary, but also bonus, equity, and advances—we can inch our way toward closing the wage gap and create a more equitable world. We can negotiate pretty much everything but most people don't. (And by the way, this is a form of community care as well.)

Before you go into your negotiation, remember your why and what you desire this money for. Also, get clear on your needs and your resentment line. There is a reason you're asking for more—remember that. Do some research ahead of time on the salary bands for the role so you are aware of what is possible. To connect this even further to your purposeful ambition, anchor your request to your gifts. Remember your exceptional abilities and how much you can impact because of them. That genius is worthy of big dollars! Practice asking for more with your friends so it's not coming out of your mouth for the first time in the negotiation.

Regulate Your Nervous System Around Money

There are many reasons our nervous systems may become dysregulated whenever finances come up. For example, we didn't grow up with money or our families had a roller-coaster relationship with it. We're pursuing money from a core wound in our desire for more. Or we find it confusing, from the ways loans and credit cards work to how to do taxes (which is all designed to be bewildering so that we stay in a state of dysregulation and uncertainty; confusion is often weaponized to perpetuate oppression). If we're dysregulated, we may sabotage ourselves if and when we do get money, because our minds and bodies don't feel safe around it. So our work is to recognize when our nervous systems are functioning suboptimally or shutting down around the conversation of money, and then regulate them.

There are many ways to regulate your nervous system, from breath work and meditation to body mapping. Try out different methods to see what works for you. And any time you're thinking about or working with money and you get anxious, use those tools. We make very different decisions when our nervous system is regulated versus when it isn't. It can be the difference between splashing out on the new wardrobe we don't need because we felt overwhelmed versus putting money in our IRA.

Exercise:
Regulate Your Nervous System
Through Body Mapping

This is a method I learned from Amy Bonaduce-Gardner.

1. Start by observing your current breath patterns for a few cycles. Notice if the breath is fast or slow, deep or shallow. Just observe.

2. Tune in to your body. When you think about money, do you feel any sensations in your body? If so, where do you feel those sensations?

3. Place awareness on the area that you feel that sensation. (If you don't feel anything in your body, choose any point you like.) Once the area is identified, commit to a precise location such as the heart or breastbone, even if you do not have an anatomical name for the location. Locate a second point nearby and then, in your mind's eye, bounce back and forth between those two points for two minutes or longer. For example, if when you think about money, you feel tightness in your heart-space, bounce your attention between the top of your heart and your breastbone (jugular notch) for two minutes or more.

4. After a few minutes you should notice a difference in your physical structure, indicating that there has been a shift in your nervous system. Do you notice anything different about your body and how you feel? (Perhaps you're sitting more upright than before. Maybe your shoulders are lower. What do you notice?)

Find the Balance Between Your Upper Limit and Never Enough

It is perfectly wonderful to desire more. Ambition is a desire for more life, as I've shared before. As an underrepresented person, it is completely ethical and rational to want a million dollars, for wealth redistribution reasons alone. Where we often get tripped up is in the "never-enough syndrome," when no amount of money is enough for us. That is when our pain is speaking. Do billionaires who are hoarding wealth *need* another billion? Nope. That mindset is exactly what has created an unhealthy and exploitative imbalance in our world.

But what is the difference between not wanting too much and having an upper limit (a false ceiling held in place by a limiting belief system)? Many of us are ping-ponging between our upper limits and never-enough syndrome. If we've hit our upper limit, chances are we're hiding and playing small. If our bank accounts are endless quarries where no amount of money will quench our desire, there is something to look at there, too. Like most things in life, there is a sweet spot somewhere in the middle, where we are expanding and taking up space in a way that aligns with our values, yet we're not so money hungry that we'll step over everyone and everything to get the extra dough. That does not a healthy relationship with ambition make.

Exercise:
Align Your Money with Purposeful Ambition

1. What were your early memories of money in childhood? What did you decide about money in that moment?

2. What did you learn about your identity and money early on? For example, that women and money are _____ or immigrants and money are _____ .

3. How was money handled in your family (or by the people who raised you)?

4. What messages were you given about work and money?

5. Was there ever emotional trauma around money for you or your family? What did you decide about money after that?

6. What were your parents' or caregivers' fears around money? Have you adopted any as your own?

7. What were your parents' or caregivers' stories around money? Have you adopted any of these as your own?

8. Is your relationship to money connected to your core wounds from chapter 1? If so, how? And how might that be impacting your current reality?

9. My current fears and stories around money are _____ .

10. I have a fear that if I had more money _____ would happen.

11. To live above the resentment line, my salary/income would need to be _____ .

12. To live above the resentment line, do you need to raise your salary or your prices? If yes: To what? And by when will you have the necessary conversations to do that?

13. Is your desire for more money connected to your purpose and your mission? If no, how can you connect those two ideas? (Note: if you feel really resistant to this there may be some limiting beliefs there.)

14. Ground your money in reality. What would you do with your new salary or income if you got it? Be specific and break down your salary into spending categories.

15. What did you learn or notice about your beliefs and habits around money?

16. Are there any limiting beliefs getting in the way? (If so, please revisit the section on limiting beliefs.)

SUPPORTING OUR NEEDS THROUGH ECONOMIC JUSTICE

It's really important to highlight that getting our needs met doesn't happen in isolation. As humans, we are interconnected and part of a system. And having our financial needs met in that system is known as "economic justice."

Economic justice is when every person has what they need to thrive, and we generate the resources together as a society. Author and coach Kelly Diels, whom I mentioned earlier, has her own three-part framework for building an economically just business model that I've always really loved: it has to be "good for self, good for the client, and good for the collective."[17] I think this framework is so helpful—particularly in the ambition conversation—and extends beyond just entrepreneurship. You can participate with your own salary or as someone who manages a budget inside an organization.

It means that we all win together, whereas the current dominant paradigm dictates that when one person wins another must lose. Our jobs should also be good for the self, for those we serve, and for the greater good. Economic justice is important because it helps us shift the focus from *I have to solve this individually* to *I get to contribute toward this as a participant while we work to solve this as a society.*

When we place the entire onus of solving money injustices (or any injustices, for that matter) on our shoulders and try to keep our prices low and prioritize others before ourselves, we often harm ourselves and limit our contributions in the process. When culture-makers who are here to drive change don't have the resources they need to thrive because they've fully taken on the burden themselves, well, that is the opposite of justice. If our work fails to exist because we've worn ourselves out by staying under-resourced and over-working, we haven't solved the problem. We, as business owners and leaders, need to be recipients of economic justice, not just providers of it. The whole point is that it's a two-way street.

Economic justice is a collective system-wide mission, and we can each be participants in and contributors to it, from being a spokesperson for an organization we deeply care about, to making regular donations, to offering scholarship spots in our group programs and digital offers, to demanding pay equity audits in our organizations, to mentorship and more. The entire point is that we contribute as a collective, so individuals don't put themselves in harm's way as we drive change.

Gabby is a freelance creative director and works with some very cool millennial-focused brands. She is the one people call when they need to make a company more culturally relevant. Gabby was recently working for a beauty brand on a limited retainer to help them revitalize their image. She had already reduced her monthly fee because she wanted this work for her portfolio. As the months went on, they asked for more work. As Gabby put her new fees (still reduced from her usual pricing) in front of the CMO, they asked if she could do more work for less money. She knew it wasn't because they didn't have the funds because Gabby was also privy to their freelance budget. They were just trying to get more for less. She said a resounding no to the request. To say yes would have put her in a challenging financial position and she'd have had to make up the lost revenue by taking on additional projects and reducing her subcontractors' fees. She would be overworked and underpaid so that a brand could have a bit more padding on its profit-and-loss statement, and that would ripple out to her team. That is not economic justice, my friends. That is exploitation.

⚘

You deserve to have all your needs met. We all do. It will look different for each of us—and it's supposed to. And when it comes to finding the sweet spot between our desire for more and what's enough, the biggest thing we want to aim for is contentment. We're going to explore that more in the next chapter.

Chapter Summary

————◇————

- You don't have to earn the right to have a need. Honoring your needs creates sustainability.

- Live above the resentment line and always be asking yourself where that line lies.

- Use the nourishment meter to find and meet your unique needs.

- Get clear on what your must-haves, nice-to-haves, and deal-breakers are for each area of your life.

- Community care and self-care are of equal importance and go hand in hand.

- A big part of getting our needs met is having enough money to do so. Get your money and make sure you're doing the work on your money story.

- Ensuring we all have enough is a system-wide effort.

Chapter 7.

PRIORITIZE CONTENTMENT

> Contentment comes from our relationship to
> what is going on around us, rather than our
> reaction to it. It is the peaceful realization that
> we are whole and complete just as we are,
> despite the anger, sadness, joy, frustration,
> and excitement that may come in and out
> from time to time.
>
> —Daniel Cordaro, PhD[1]

One of the challenging misconceptions about ambitious folks is that nothing is ever enough for us, that we'll never be content. But remember, this is a hallmark of *painful ambition* only. When we are striving from a place of pain, no amount of money, titles, accolades, or *New York Times* bestsellers will ever be enough. Why? Because we're trying to solve for internal wounds with arbitrary external measures. It doesn't work. Believe me, I've tried. You probably have, too. And so have many others.

Instead, we have to find contentment, which asks us to find the wholeness within before we turn outward toward what we want. It offers a more sustainable and fulfilling approach to life.

CHOOSING CONTENTMENT OVER HAPPINESS

The West is obsessed with the notion of happiness. In fact, a quick search on Amazon results in over twenty thousand book titles purporting to help us find this elusive state, showing just how strong our desire for it is. Yet while happiness and contentment are often used interchangeably and do operate in sync, they are actually quite distinct—one fuels purposeful ambition much more than the other.

On one hand, happiness is the feeling of pleasure or satisfaction we experience from outcomes in our life, such as accomplishments or milestones. Because it's an emotion, it's therefore temporary. Contentment, on the other hand, is a state of inner peace that sustains us regardless of external circumstances. While the pursuit of happiness has us constantly chasing a moving goalpost, contentment allows us to be with what is while being open to more. In other words, happiness is fleeting; contentment is stable.

In life we want both happiness *and* contentment, though most of us tend to focus on happiness alone. This is a fool's errand because human emotions are naturally transitory. It's unfeasible to feel happy all the time. The pressure to always be happy just leads to disappointment because it's simply not a human possibility. If we set goals according to what we think may make us happy, it's unlikely that we'll reach genuine fulfillment.

In fact, Dr. Robert Lustig, professor emeritus of pediatrics at University of California, San Francisco, believes that our pursuit of happiness is actually making us miserable. In his book *The Hacking of the American Mind*, he underscores that as a society, we're conflating happiness, pleasure, and contentment, and it's causing real friction.[2] The desire for more "likes," new luxury items, and the next promotion is driven by our quest for dopamine, the neuro-transmitter responsible for motivation and pursuit,[3] and this perpetual chase can lead to addiction. In other words, as a society, we've become hooked on short-term pleasure.

Of course, happiness isn't a bad thing; we just need to release our overdependence on it and make space for other emotions. When "the world's first happiness hacker" Penny Locaso interviewed more than one hundred study participants ranging in age from twenty-two to seventy, she found those who were feeling most fulfilled were those who let themselves feel and process the emotions we usually label as negative—like sadness, fear, and resentment—alongside the more optimistic ones.[4] Suppressing emotions such as anger, grief, and frustration can harm us because when we repress any parts of our feelings, we deny the fullness of our human experience. And as we learned from the section on shadows, when we deny one feeling, we also suppress its polar opposite.

We need to feel the positive and the challenges as they provide data about our lives and our experiences that inform how we navigate life. Experiencing a range of emotions is known as emodiversity.[5] Unfortunately, many of us feel like we aren't allowed to bring all of our emotions to the table. Think of the tropes of the villainous Arab, the hysterical female, or the angry Black man that lead many people in those groups to suppress their anger. But pushing down our emotions to make others comfortable only harms us in the process. We all should get to experience the full range of our emotions—and it's healthy to do so. Studies show that allowing yourself to feel a range of emotions is correlated with decreased depression, doctor visits, and medical bills.[6] In other words, when we allow ourselves to feel and experience all of our feelings, good and bad, we can have a more honest conversation with our ambition.

While the US tends to prioritize happiness, in many Eastern traditions, contentment is considered the most favorable state. Researching five thousand years of human philosophy and two hundred years of scientific research, Dr. Daniel Cordaro—founder and CEO of the Contentment Foundation—pored over material from ancient wisdom traditions, and to his shock, these traditions rarely used the word "happiness." In fact, what he found was that more than 90 percent of the time, the word "contentment" was used. It was described as "unconditional wholeness" regardless of what is happening externally.[7] Moreover, when Cordaro's team of University of Chicago researchers were studying emotions in Eastern Bhutan, their guide, Dr. Dorji Wangchuk, shared just how special this state of being is: "It's hard to translate [contentment] exactly, but the closest word is *chokkshay*, which is a very deep and spiritual word that means 'the knowledge of enough.'"[8] In essence, it means that we have the awareness that what we have right here, right now, is whole and complete.

That unconditional wholeness we feel allows us to be in a more purposeful relationship with ambition. We are not seeking external things like jobs, awards, or big titles to make us whole. The wholeness comes from within. How incredible is that? Instead of anchoring ourselves to transient feelings, we can be in the present and allow that to be enough. Rather than looking for what could be, we can be here with and accepting of what is in the moment.

Something my nervous-system coach Amy Bonaduce-Gardner taught me is that when we take ourselves out of the present and into future or past states—whether that's through worrying about a presentation we have tomorrow or revisiting the embarrassment we felt when we made a mistake at work last year—we actually send our bodies into fight or flight. The fight-or-flight brain sees what is the same in our current reality and compares it to the past to understand the present or predict the future. This takes us on a sympathetic path that has little to do with what is happening now and can then keep us stuck and rob us of the opportunity for novel experiences, ideas, and learning.

If I intentionally dwell on the past or future, this creates a discrepancy between my unconscious brain (whose job it is to take in and process sensory information about my present moment) and my conscious brain (whose job it is to make decisions based on the sensory input revealed by the unconscious brain but that is now thinking about a different moment entirely). When the reality in my head doesn't match the reality of my external environment, my sympathetic nervous system is activated—better safe than sorry!

Contentment not only allows us to be present, it invites our nervous system into a state of rest and digest. According to Bonaduce-Gardner, the rest-and-digest, or parasympathetic, brain we have while in a state of contentment "notices the uniqueness in each moment, informs us how this is different from yesterday, and approaches tomorrow with a sense of curiosity." This allows us to meet the reality of the moment. We may have just received a triggering email, but there is no actual lion in the room chasing us.

CULTIVATE YOUR CONTENTMENT

While a perpetual chase for happiness can keep us on a painful ambition treadmill, contentment allows us to answer the question *When is enough enough?* Let's look at how we can begin to cultivate a contentment that draws us closer to purposeful ambition. The first step is to design our lives around what we value.

Align Your Work with Your Values

As we learned in chapter 4, your core values are the guiding standards for your life. Your values allow you to enter a partnership, workplace, project, friendship, or community and ask, *Do we care about the same things? And how much does that matter to each of us?* If an organization's core values are in direct contrast to your own, there will come a time when the organization eventually asks you to abandon or compromise a part of yourself, sometimes forcing you to hide behind the same masks you clung to in childhood. In doing so, you will violate your purposeful ambition.

This happened to my client Patricia, who was the VP of sales and marketing for an athleisure brand for several years. Though she enjoyed her team very much, she didn't feel like she was learning and growing, which was one of her core values. But she was so torn because she didn't want to leave her team in the lurch. Every day, she worried that she wasn't as sharp as she used to be because her role didn't stretch her in the ways she wanted. At first, she let it go because the team was kind and supportive. But bit by bit, a little voice crept in reminding her of how much she loved learning, and how little her current role allowed her to do so. She sought out external growth opportunities, but it didn't feel the same. She was in a place of stagnation with her growth but was also sacrificing her dreams by staying there for the sake of her team.

Eventually, the voice became louder and impossible to ignore. Work stopped feeling additive, and Patricia began to resent it. She couldn't show up authentically, nor could she bring the fullness of her gifts to the table. How can we ever be in a good relationship with our ambition when we are effectively hiding who we are? It was when the resentment edged in that Patricia decided it was time to find a job that prioritized her growth and development. (And she did. And they gave her a large learning and development stipend. A win-win.)

Values alignment at work is so important, studies have shown that when it's not there, we often need to raise other factors to feel more fulfilled. For example, when researchers Paul Ingram and Yoonjin Choi analyzed chief operating officers, they found that when COOs were not aligned with the company's values, they needed a *40 percent raise* to feel more satisfied with their work.[9] I've seen this with my clients, too. When work doesn't feel connected to what matters for them, they overuse monetary compensation as a way to feel more nourished. Meaning is missing from their work and they're trying to find it financially. But that is a short-term strategy because money alone doesn't lead to contentment; we need to share values with our workplaces in order to thrive.

To determine if your work is currently aligned with your values, you first have to get clear on what your values are. Let's use the exercise on the following page.

What Ingram and Choi's deep research around values has concluded is that when a company's values match the values of its employees, the entire operation unfolds with much more ease. There tends to be greater job satisfaction, less attrition, healthier and more supportive communication, stronger contributions, and a greater sense of belonging. Companies should feel incentivized to encourage values alignment.

Exercise:
Find Your Values

EXAMPLE VALUES

Justice	Reliability	Consistency
Commitment	Open-Mindedness	Innovation
Honesty/Radical Candor	Efficiency	Compassion/Kindness
Creativity	Good Humor	Positivity
Spirit of Adventure	Motivation	Respect
Optimism	Passion (Spark)	Education
Fitness	Courage	Service to Others
Perseverance	Equality	Joy
Environmentalism	Loyalty	Freedom
Women's Empowerment	Gender Justice	Connection

1. Looking at this list, what are your core values? If you were to distill your values down to the top five most important for you, what would they be?

2. If you're having a hard time readily pointing to your values, think of a time recently when you had an upsetting interaction. What values were absent?

3. What values do you want to ensure are carried through your work?

4. If you work within an organization, what values do you need the organization to uphold in order for you to feel in alignment?

5. What values do you want to embody in a deeper way in your current role?

6. How can you start to get on the court with those values today?

Sort Through Your Expectations

What we expect of ourselves and others can often preclude our contentment. When I first started my business, I assumed entrepreneurship was like school: you get out what you put in, and if you study and do all the things you're "supposed to," you'll get an A and achieve your goals. Goodness, did the universe give me a slap when I first started! Entrepreneurship taught me, more than any other practice, that you don't always get out what you put in, and that circumstances aren't always fair. My first year as a founder was a very disappointing one, and as a child of trauma, the first thing I did was tell myself a story that I wasn't good at this and something was inherently wrong with me. Of course, the reality was there was nothing wrong with me. My expectations were simply way out of whack.

The expectations other people may place on us can also have an impact on our contentment. Perhaps your manager expects you to deliver a close-to-perfect work product, even if you're juggling several projects at once and may not have the time to polish your work. Or your team expects immediate feedback despite you having a calendar full of meetings. Or your coworkers expect you to answer calls and emails on weekends, which is just not possible with the demands of your own schedule. Being aware of these expectations can be both a help and a hindrance to our contentment: It's helpful in the sense that we know what people want and need, and a hindrance in that the weight of these expectations can lead us to perform far beyond our capacity versus setting boundaries for our own needs.

The reality is expectations are everywhere. We can't avoid them, but we can learn to work with them. The trick is to aim them high enough ("enough" being the operative word here) that we're operating within our growth edge, and to surrender to the outcome. For example, I would love for this book to be a bestseller but my contentment doesn't depend on it. My deeper goal is to write a book that will change your life and give that process my all. I can't control the end result.

Setting realistic expectations has been a hard-won lesson for many of my ambitious clients because, oftentimes, those expectations are not aligned with their true why. Grace, for example, was a high-potential employee at one of the world's top consulting firms. She told me that as one of the few Asian Americans in her group, she felt "a tremendous amount of pressure to prove herself" and achieve success at a lightning-fast speed. In her mid-thirties, she was short-listed for partnership at the firm, which was a huge feat in and of itself; this can take about fifteen years, meaning most consultants don't make partner until forty at the earliest. With only a few other female Asian partners in the entire industry, Grace was hell-bent on getting there early.

In the grueling process it takes to interview for a partnership, Grace doubled down, gave up her weekends, and even hired a speaking coach to prepare for the review committee. She did what she does best: overprepare and outwork her competitors. She made it through the first set of interviews. But after the second round, she was informed she didn't make it. She called me, devastated, confused, but most of all angry. As we explored her anger, it became abundantly clear Grace was angry with herself. She was a make-it-happen kind of woman. How was she not able to bring this to fruition?

We started by looking at Grace's why, her reason for making partner in the first place. Thinking this through, she realized she had wanted to become one of the youngest female Asian partners in the industry in order to feel valuable and worthy, and to show her parents, colleagues, and peers that she was capable. Her desire to win, not her true purpose or values, was what was driving her. By now we know this is a hallmark of painful ambition, and not the way to reach contentment.

It wasn't until we had this very real conversation about expectations, both her own and her parents', that Grace realized how out of alignment she was. She expected that twisting herself into the image of what she thought a partner should be would win her the role. But inside that expectation was a very hard truth: she wasn't being her real self to get there. Making partner was actually her parents' dream, not her own. Grace started reevaluating everything and eventually stepped away from consulting and into the health care industry, which she had always been passionate about.

When it comes to examining the expectations we've placed on ourselves, we want to ask, like Grace, *What is the true intent behind our desire?* Expectations are rarely our own ideas. They are usually placed on us by our families and communities, even by managers. Coming back to our why can help center us in purposeful ambition. If our intention is to chase more because that's what the world expects of us, we're likely in painful ambition. If our intention is to grow and further unfold from each experience, we're likely in a more purposeful relationship. Orienting our expectations around our true intent opens up a whole new, more contented, and more purposeful way of being. Keep coming back to your why.

Use the below exercise to ensure you are more connected to your intentions than to the expectations of others.

Exercise:
Align Your Expectations with Your Intentions

1. List out a few goals you're currently working toward.

2. For each of the goals you listed, identify why you want to achieve each of them.

3. Are they connected to your mission and purpose that we named in chapter 4?

4. If these goals aren't connected to your mission and purpose, whose goals are they? And has chasing them impacted your contentment?

5. How can you shift these goals to be more aligned?

6. It can feel really uncomfortable to give up something we've been working toward, even if it's someone else's expectation of us. What would need to happen for you to feel more comfortable doing so?

Stop Playing the Comparison Game

Nothing robs us of our contentment quite like comparison.

Now, before any of you go and shame yourselves for comparing yourself to others, I want to remind you: it's completely natural to do so. Most of us compare and despair. Comparison is the simplest way we come to understand ourselves, what we're great at, and what we aren't. According to social comparison theory, it's also how we as humans determine our personal and social value. But it's when we reside too long in that place of comparison that causes us harm, because comparison skews our perception of ourselves. And there are few things that affect us more than social media. In fact, the usage of multiple social media platforms has been linked to an increase in depression and anxiety symptoms because we're constantly assessing ourselves against people's highlight reels.[10]

Our families, too, can be a breeding ground for comparison. This was especially true for Halé, my client. Halé is an exceptional woman—a celebrated entrepreneur, gifted artist, and well-loved friend—but she couldn't see any of that. She grew up in a family where her older sister was the golden child because she fit the more standard definition of "genius" with her high IQ scores and straight A's. Growing up, Halé's mother and grandmother often measured her against her sister in big and small ways, like how many friends she had, her waist circumference, and the number of awards she won. Because Halé was always up against someone else's standard of success, she often felt like a loser.

When she told me that, I was blown away. Here was a woman who, for all intents and purposes, was wildly loved and appreciated, and who had achieved a whole lot of success. But because someone else had set the bar, and the bar was to be exactly like her sister, she always felt like she was falling short. This really got in the way of Halé feeling any kind of contentment.

The truth is, we can never be successful at being anyone but ourselves. If we design our lives from a place of comparison, we live as captives to other people's choices. When society tells us there is one standard or preferred way of being, it's literally a lie designed to make us feel small. Your only job (and it is a big job!) is to be the *you*-est you.

Sadly, like Halé, a lot of us come from a lineage of comparison.

If someone in our family doesn't feel good enough, they often project their insecurities onto us, and then we carry those ideas with us as if they were our own. Over time, Halé was able to cultivate compassion for her mother and grandmother because they, too, had lived this way. They had also had expectations placed on them and had been taught that life is a competition where we have to continually fight to measure up. What a challenging way to live!

When we feel secure and confident about ourselves, we are less likely to keep tabs on others. For instance, one study looked at both happy and sad participants and asked each person to compare themselves to a peer who was "better" or "worse" off than them. Sad participants felt worse when matched with a better peer, and better when matched with a worse peer. Happy people, on the other hand, were much less affected by who they were compared to.[11] If we find ourselves in a cycle of comparing ourselves to others, it's important to come back to ourselves and ask, *Where am I not feeling good about me?*

That said, there are times when comparison can be constructive—but it depends on what we choose to do with that information. For instance, I often tell my clients that jealousy can be a helpful emotion because it points us to what we admire in others that is also inherent in ourselves, but that we have yet to express. For example, if you're jealous of your colleague's speaking career, it may highlight that you also have that gift and want to be on a stage sharing it. If we use that insight to explore our relationship to striving and then refine our lives, it can be supportive. However, if we simply stew in the comparison, it keeps us far from contentment.

One of the best ways to shift out of comparison is to focus on your own gifts and how you want to use them in service. It's much harder to be lost in comparison when we are captivated by our own purpose. Your responsibility in this life is to honor your own internal desire for growth—the key being, of course, that this tug comes from the inside, not the outside. When we are clear on who we are and what our contribution to the world is, and are continually refining it, we have less energy to devote to holding up a measuring stick to others. Putting down our expectations and comparisons allows us to be more ourselves, more real. When we spend our lives reacting from our pain, we never let our souls speak.

Exercise:
Shift Out of Comparison

1. Where and how am I comparing myself to others? What feelings is this bringing up in me?

2. Can I use these feelings to refine how I'm showing up in my own life? What can I learn from these feelings?

3. Is there something unexpressed in me that wishes to come through? Where am I not being fully myself?

4. How do I need to change my relationship to social media (or other media) to reduce my unhelpful comparison?

5. Own your greatness by making a list of five things that make you special and unique. Spend a few minutes each day celebrating these gifts.

6. Make a list of the ways you can go deeper with your gifts versus focusing on others.

Invest in Aligned Community

When it comes to achieving contentment in work and life, ensuring we have aligned community around us is of vital importance. This isn't just about having a certain number of relationships, but about engaging in ones that are truly meaningful and supportive. Healthy relationships have been shown to lead to a stronger immune system, longevity, and increased resilience to stress, while some studies suggest that they can actually reduce our risk of mortality.[12]

Yet one of the biggest areas my clients struggle with is interpersonal relationships, and it's often because they are investing in the wrong people.

A few years ago, I was working with a woman named Theresa. She was an awesome, superaccomplished executive and mother who always put her family first—even her extended family. One day she came to our call bereft. Her sister-in-law had been speaking poorly of her in the next room. She didn't realize Theresa was in earshot and heard the whole thing. What made Theresa most upset is that she prided herself on being good to her family. She bent over backward to help them with errands, get them gifts they would truly enjoy, and be kind. But no matter what she did, her sister-in-law always seemed to have something negative to say about her.

Hearing Theresa's story sparked a realization for me: *We don't have to show up for everyone like they are our everything.* Not everyone asks for that kind of relationship. In fact, we often assume it's what they want and place that expectation on them ourselves.

After our session, I took out my journal and thought about the people I loved most in the world and want to show up fully for. The list was short. Then I thought about the people I really like and want to support, but to whom I don't give an all-access pass. The list was a little longer, but not by much. Next, I reflected on who I'd consider to be acquaintances, the people I was still getting to know. This was the longest list. I eventually created a five-part framework to decide how I wanted to show up for my community.

Our community has five levels:

1. The ones: These are our *people* who we will do anything and everything for, and they would do the same for us.

2. The twos: The twos are great! We really like them, but we don't need to be around them all the time.

3. The threes: These folks are just fine. We might still be establishing a connection with them. At this point they don't inspire our greatness, but they don't send us into a frenzy, either.

4. The fours: They are not aligned with our values and drain our energy.

5. The fives: The fives are unhealthy for us to be around because they are so depleting or misaligned.

AUTHENTIC COMMUNITY

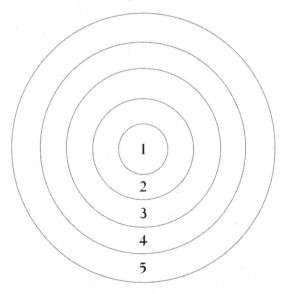

Sometimes our ambitious nature can spill over into our relationships, and we feel like we have to be the best at friendship in order to matter. But this is a dishonest approach that often breeds resentment. The reality is, we don't have unlimited time and energy to spend on every single person in our orbit. Not everyone gets an all-access pass to the amazingness that we are. We get to *choose* who we want in our inner circle and who we would rather keep at arm's length. This isn't about weighing and measuring people or playing a game of tit for tat. It's about getting really honest about who we want in our lives, how we want to show up for them, and how we'd like them to show up for us. We get to apply the same purposeful framework to our friendships and relationships as we do to our work, to ensure our relationships are truly aligned with who we are and what we really want.

My session with Theresa gave way to the following exercise on identifying your aligned community.

Exercise:
Identify Your Aligned Community

I invite you to be agile around this as it will most likely shift over time. These aren't hard-and-fast rules but a framework that supports community and contentment.

1. **WHO**
   Identify who in your life falls into the ones, twos, threes, fours, and fives.

   * The ones:
   * The twos:
   * The threes:

- The fours:
- The fives:

2. **HOW**

How do you want to show up for each of these groups? What do you give them? What parts of *you* can they access?

How frequently do you want to connect with each group?

- The ones:
- The twos:
- The threes:
- The fours:
- The fives:

3. **WHAT**

What do you want to have on the receiving end from these groups? How do you expect them to treat you? How do they show up for you?

- The ones:
- The twos:
- The threes:
- The fours:
- The fives:

4. How does all of this feel? Does this feel empowering or does this feel triggering? Why? Are there any limiting beliefs keeping you stuck or small here?

5. Do you need to have any boundary-setting conversations with your community to honor this framework?

Aligned community doesn't just create greater contentment for us—it allows us to extend that experience out into the world. In the words of Deepa Purushothaman, "To profoundly change the system and sustain our personal power, we also need the 'power of we.' We need to find others to feed our strength, to know we are not alone, and to be witnesses to our struggles so we can be fully seen."[13]

My client Kate, who is a Buddhist meditation teacher, author, and social justice activist, says, "We can look at friendship as a spiritual practice and one that helps us to develop and enrich our inner lives and also that we can support one another on a common path to liberation."[14] We cannot do this work alone, and the most profound and meaningful connections, the ones that see us and hold us most deeply, can be the most transformative. An eighty-five-year Harvard study found the number one thing that makes us fulfilled in life is strong friendships and community.[15] They can assuage our fears by reminding us of our greatness. They can encourage our bravery through their own. They can help us shift culture by taking risks and being the change right alongside us. Contentment and purposeful ambition requires the "power of we"[16] and that we get really honest with ourselves about who is included in that we.

Practice the Art of Play

Growing up, my mother was severely under-resourced as she raised five children while my dad worked long hours and grappled with his mental health. Seeing her struggle, I quickly took on a more adult role and dove into caregiving. I would get my sisters ready for school, pick them up in the afternoon, and do their homework with them. I would cook and clean, filling in the parenting gaps. I got something out of it, too. It's how I derived my feelings of worthiness and maintained my status as "the good girl." But as you can imagine, this didn't leave a lot of time to be a child, which carried over into my work life later on.

As an adult, I received a lot of feedback about being "all work and no play." One day, frustrated to hear that for about the thousandth time, I hired a creativity coach. In our first session together, they asked me to set up "play stations" in my apartment. Hearing this, I had a mini existential crisis and immediately felt annoyed. "What do you mean, to play in?" I pushed. "What does that even look like?" They gave me a virtual tour of their space to show me their pockets of play. There was a drumming station. A place where they would dance. A journaling nook. An easel set up for painting. They invited me to explore what that would look like for me.

At first, I felt so awkward. I had no idea how to play or where to begin. I ambled over to my local pharmacy, a Duane Reade just down the block, and went to the stationery section. I bought some glitter markers, a Spirograph set (do you remember those sets of rings and wheels that we'd trace and make designs out of?), and a sketchbook. I went home, sat on the floor and emptied out my bag, and began to fuss with the items. After about ten minutes, I glanced down at my messy scribbles and peeled the page out of my sketchbook. It was ugly and I didn't like it.

Every week for three months I'd meet my creativity coach on Zoom while they attempted to return me to my inner child who knew how to take a stick and a rock and make a game out of it—the one who didn't care if things were perfect as long as they were fun. I resisted it so hard. I spent at least the first month fighting my coach and my nature. And then something shifted. I started to see the power of play by what was unfolding from our sessions. I started to feel less stressed and agitated. When I felt bored but didn't want to work, I had a place to go. I was laughing more. I felt free to be silly. I was able to be in the present moment, because play demands we be with what is in front of us.

Numerous studies underscore the power of play. It can reduce our stress levels by releasing endorphins, and boost our well-being by contributing to an overall feeling of joy.[17] It can enhance our relationships.[18] It can even increase our creativity.[19] Yet so many of us have no idea how to play. The good news is, there is no wrong way to do it!

One good place to start is by looking at the four main styles of play, as defined by professor and psychology researcher Dr. René Proyer: other-directed, lighthearted, intellectual, and whimsical. Other-directed play is playing with others. This can look like a game of badminton or saying yes to a game your friend made up. Those with a lighthearted play style may love a more relaxed style of play, where participants are free to improvise and are not worried about outcomes. I once attended a kirtan, a call-and-response form of chanting that is part of the Hare Krishna movement, Hinduism, Sikhism, Buddhism, and various other traditions. In this chanting, the person leading would frequently change their tone and tempo. I saw that as lighthearted play because it incorporated improvisation, and no one was worried about sounding perfect. Intellectual players love to solve problems and use critical thinking in their play, such as in whodunit games, while whimsical players prefer "extraordinary or unusual things," such as fairy-tale-inspired play.[20] The invitation here is to find your ideal version of play and engage in it without any expectations or masks, tapping into your inner child and allowing them to direct these free-flowing activities without the need for your ego to do the driving.

Now, I know what you're going to say: *I don't have time to sleep, let alone play.* But like meditation, I would argue that we can't afford *not* to play. Even five minutes a day can contribute to our contentment. Like when cultivating our genius, we want to start with just a few minutes each day and let that grow over time. All work and no play perpetuates painful ambition—take it from me.

Here are a few ideas for how you might incorporate play into your everyday:

- Play a question game with your kids, nieces, nephews, or even coworkers. Play twenty questions or two truths and a lie. (This is one of my faves and how I earned the title of "the fun auntie"!)

- Set up a creativity station in your home. Get some markers and a sketchpad, knitting needles and yarn, beads and thread, or whatever strikes your fancy. Set a five-minute timer to just create.

- Put together a playlist that you cannot help but dance around to. Set a timer to dance it out at least five minutes a day. Extra credit if you allow it be weird and uncoordinated and just let your inner child do the moving!

- Invite your friends to a monthly game night. Buy a game such as Cards Against Humanity or a murder mystery that's easy for multiple people to enjoy.

For many of us ambitious folks who haven't given ourselves permission to play in decades, the notion of play can kick up our competitive side. If your tendency is to play to win, ask yourself why. What meaning are you making of winning or losing?

Then ask yourself, *What would it be like to play for the joy of it instead?*

⁂

I n a world that prioritizes happiness, it can feel countercultural to prioritize contentment over happiness. I remember when I first read about contentment, there was a part of me that felt a twinge of sadness. I wondered, *Does this mean I'll never feel the high-highs of delight?* Hopefully by the end of this chapter you know it doesn't mean that at all. Focusing on contentment means we've made space for joy as well as for uncomfortable feelings, for community, and for our values to be centered. And in all of that, we've maintained a state of inner peace and satisfaction that we feel regardless of what is happening around us. It's a deep knowing that even if everything falls apart, we will still have our inner stability to keep us sound.

Chapter Summary

- Contentment is "unconditional wholeness" based on the "knowledge of enough."

- In life we need both contentment and happiness, but they are not the same. Allow happiness to come and go. Attempting to grip on to this transient state is making us miserable.

- The most contented people allow for emodiversity— which means experiencing a range of emotions.

- Building our lives around our values supports higher contentment.

- Step out of comparison and expectations. Both things are eroding your contentment.

- Study after study suggests that aligned community contributes to greater contentment and well-being. Choose your people discerningly.

- Don't forget to play!

Chapter 8.

TAKE ALIGNED ACTION

I want a big life. I want to experience everything.
I want to break every single rule there is. They
say ambition is an unattractive trait in a
woman. . . . But you know what's really
unattractive? Waiting around for something to
happen. Staring out a window, thinking the life
you should be living is out there somewhere but
not being willing to open the door and go get it.
Even if someone tells you you can't. Being a
coward is only cute in *The Wizard of Oz*.

—MRS. MAISEL, *The Marvelous Mrs. Maisel*[1]

When I first started my coaching business, my only
goals were to leverage my gifts and replace my marketing salary. At first, that felt nearly impossible.
How could I quickly replace earnings I had spent almost a decade
working up to? I started with one coaching client who came to me
via my network. But then I added another, and another. Every day
I moved closer toward the dream. And over the course of a year, I
was able to replace my previous income.

Once I did that, more things felt possible, so I set my sights on hiring an assistant and paying them well. Done. Then I felt ready to solidify some larger corporate contracts. I checked that box, too. And when I did, I needed a bigger team. So I made that happen as well. Eventually I was ready to write a book—and now you know how that one went.

My point is, it takes one healthy ambitious step at a time to transform our lives into something unrecognizable and wildly beautiful. You have within and around you all the skills, brilliance, and community you need to get yourself out of an ill-fitting situation and into your most scintillating future. Life *is* unfair *and* we can still have our wildest dreams. All of this can be true at once. If my clients and I can do it, so can you. Because all of us are just as extraordinary as the next person.

In this chapter, we're going to explore how to set goals that are aligned with our purposeful ambition and that can lead us toward our most fulfilling lives, and then build habits to help us meet them. In the process, we're dropping the shoulds and must-dos that usually drive our goals, and instead we're letting our truth and purpose take the lead. The first step is to determine whether our goals are ones that stretch us and are therefore psychologically safe and kind, and uphold purposeful ambition. Let's go through each of these one by one. Ready?

IS YOUR GOAL PSYCHOLOGICALLY SAFE?

Remember this image from a few chapters ago?

It illustrates the three zones we operate in: our comfort zone, where it feels safe but we are not evolving; our stretch zone, where we are on the growth edge; and the panic zone, where we've gone

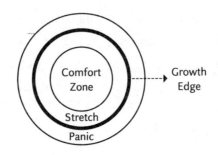

	Psychological Safety	Accountability
Comfort	High	Low
Stretch	High	High
Panic	Low	High

Based on the Zone Model by Karl Rohnke

past our growth edge and tipped into fear, anxiety, and sometimes sheer terror. As we learned, we want to spend plenty of time in the stretch zone, where there is a high degree of accountability so we actually do what we say we're going to do, but, most important, where there is a significant sense of psychological safety so we feel secure enough to take risks. We don't need to live here though. Amazing things happen in the stretch zone, but it isn't sustainable to expand all the time. Think about the diagram I shared in the introduction about ambition being like a perennial flower. Sometimes our ambition is the seedling growing underground. Occasionally it needs to rest and recover, which is akin to the comfort zone. Stretching all the time can be a form of painful ambition. But when it is time to stretch, psychological safety is a necessary component of healthy forward movement and is therefore essential to preserving healthy ambition.

My client Isla's experience underscores why psychological safety is so important. Isla was a human resources executive at a global food manufacturer and had spent the last few years focused on learning and development for their vast international workforce. It sparked a light in her. So much so that now there was a kernel of desire for her to start her own coaching practice and work with career pivoters outside of her company. In three months, we designed her curriculum, coaching offer, sales and marketing strategy, and everything else she needed to start the business.

Initially, Isla had planned to leave her full-time job and jump straight into her coaching practice. But when it came time to part ways with her employer, she tipped straight into the panic zone. Leaving was too big a leap for her nervous system. She was flooded with dread and was unable to take action. So, we designed a more psychologically safe way for her to launch her business. We outlined a minimal viable offer that would allow her to test the strength of her coaching program while also maintaining her full-time job, and Isla opened up only three spots for coaching. This way, she felt safe to make and learn from mistakes. We then set revenue goals and key metrics that, when reached, would signal it was time for Isla to leave her day job and step fully into the business. Now, don't get me wrong—she still had moments where she questioned herself and felt out of her depth. But in those moments, she leaned into me for accountability and support, and continued to take one psychologically safe step at a time.

I once worked with a coach who said they were not "in the business of safety." I get what they meant. They wanted people to be bold and do things that scared them—and I do, too. But there is a sweet spot. If we're petrified, it can feel impossible to take action because our bodies are in a state of fight, flight, freeze, or fawn. We either avoid the growth, sabotage ourselves, freeze and do nothing, or go back to chasing our bigness from a place of pain because it's what we know best. Psychological safety, and feeling secure in our bodies and nervous systems, is necessary for making lasting change.

IS YOUR GOAL KIND?

Most of us are used to setting SMART goals: goals that are specific, measurable, achievable, relevant, and time-bound. This body of work was originated by George Doran, in his 1981 article "There's a S.M.A.R.T. Way to Write Management's Goals and Objectives," but has since been criticized as unhelpful and even counterintuitive.[2] While I believe that some of those qualifiers are supportive around our goals, I want to layer in an additional idea.

A lot of times when we set goals, we forget to ask, *Is this a kind thing for me to ask of myself?* Our ambition has us chasing the biggest thing we can set our sights on, and we forget to check in and see if this is aligned for us and the life we want to lead. So a question I often ask clients when they're setting goals is, *Is this kind?* The word "kind" has Old English and Proto-Germanic roots meaning "natural" and "compassionate."[3] When we're setting goals for ourselves, are they so big that they ask something unnatural of us? Does the stretch require something so intense that there is the absence of compassion? Meeting our goals should never come at the expense of ourselves.

A few years ago, my client Leila set a goal of taking her business from $400,000 a year to the $1 million mark. When we sat down and did the math of what would need to happen in order to reach this goal, the road there wasn't looking so compassionate. As a consultant, Leila's average engagement was $25,000 per project.

Her closing rate when she got on sales calls was 40 percent. That meant that she would need to close forty clients and have one hundred sales calls in one year to meet that goal. Normally, she booked about four or five sales calls a month, so she would effectively need to double that. What I didn't tell you about Leila is that she was also newly diagnosed with an autoimmune disease and was in the process of getting divorced.

As a coach, I'm just there to hold up a mirror. It's not my job to tell someone if a goal is the right size for them or not. In fact, it's of the utmost importance that my clients decide that for themselves. Otherwise, they are just outsourcing their decisions and ambition again. So after we did the math and looked at everything else going on in Leila's life, I asked her, "Is this kind?" And as I asked it, she immediately started to weep. She had initially set the million-dollar goal because that is where she felt her next big milestone "should" be. But this year, what she really wanted was to take amazing care of herself. She was going through a lot personally, and she wanted to spend more time giving back to herself than she wanted to spend in sales calls. She still wanted to grow her revenue, as that would help her invest in self-care, but when she saw what was required to get her to the million-dollar mark, she realized it wasn't the healthiest goal for this season of her life.

The idea of kindness is not anti-ambition or anti-goal. I am an advocate for you getting all that you desire. In fact, I'm often encouraging my clients in the direction of *bigger* and *more* because their limiting beliefs have them asking for too little. One client even calls me the "queen of delulu" because I want her to dream so expansively. But kindness and compassion should be a huge factor in how we go about getting what we want. Leila didn't want those million dollars if it came at the expense of her well-being and mental health—it felt unkind given what was happening in the rest of her life. So she adjusted her revenue target to $600,000 and then set a goal to take amazing care of herself this year, which included working out with a personal trainer, regular therapy, a beautiful meal delivery service, and incorporating a weekly date with herself and friends to have fun, like taking a ceramics class or roller-skating.

DOES YOUR GOAL HONOR PURPOSEFUL AMBITION?

When it comes to setting healthy goals, we also want to make sure they are aligned with our purposeful ambition and not coming from a place of pain. Remember the chart from chapter 1 on purposeful ambition versus painful ambition? As you think about your goals, go through each aspect of painful and purposeful ambition to see whether each goal aligns with the truth of who you are—or if you're pursuing it because society tells us it's the next big milestone.

PURPOSEFUL AMBITION: A CONSCIOUS RELATIONSHIP WITH AMBITION	PAINFUL AMBITION: AN UNCONSCIOUS RELATIONSHIP WITH AMBITION
Questioning systems that shape our ambition: Instead of being unaware of the systems and ideologies that have molded us, you question them. You recognize that the starting line is not the same for all of us.	**Unaware of the systems that shape our ambition:** You are unconscious of the systems that have shaped you and the people around you. You believe we all have equal opportunities to get where we want to go.

An expansive mindset:	A narrow mindset:
• You realize that each opportunity in our lives is a chance to grow and that perfection is a myth.	• You fear failure. You are perfectionistic and unforgiving of flaws in yourself and others.
• You question your limiting beliefs.	• You think in black-and-white/either-or ways.
• You lead with vulnerability and compassion.	• You have a tendency to live from your limiting beliefs. You lead with judgment.
• You are centered in abundance.	
• You actively work to validate and honor yourself. You depend on internal validation.	• You are coming from a place of scarcity.
	• You are driven by a need to be seen, heard, and validated by others. You depend on external validation.
Driven by purpose: Instead of being focused on just winning no matter the cost, you have a desire to connect to purpose, make a positive impact, and change what's broken, and an eagerness to grow from a place of wholeness. You make choices based on alignment.	**Driven by winning no matter the cost:** You have a desire to win and succeed for acclaim, or to be liked, and a need to be the best. You are driven to succeed based on feelings of inadequacy. You make choices based on the shoulds.
Focused on collaboration and using your gifts to help the world: You understand and leverage your gifts for the greater good instead of being focused on the competition. You are all about collaboration, diversity, equity, and community.	**Focused on individualism and hoarding power:** You are all about the self and shining as an individual. You believe acclaim and resources are scarce or for the select few, so you amass these for yourself.
Honoring your needs: You are in loving collaboration with your mind and body. You center your care and the care of your community. You do not instrumentalize yourself.	**Instrumentalizing yourself and others:** You overuse your mind and body to get ahead. You dehumanize yourself and others. You are self-sacrificing.

Contentment-based: You welcome all emotions and experiences and focus on equanimity, rejecting toxic positivity.	**Living in toxic positivity:** You perpetually seek happiness only, avoiding or denying challenging emotions.
Take aligned action: • You move at the speed of trust. You are conscious of deadlines and dependencies but honor the people and processes it takes to create great work. • You prioritize psychological safety over speed and fear.	**Self-imposed urgency:** • You move at an unsustainable pace to prove yourself and your efficiency. • You move based on fear, inciting panic in yourself and others. You are motived by fear-based tactics.

Exercise:
Set Psychologically Safe, Kind, and Purposeful Goals

1. What goals did you set and achieve last year? Plan a little celebration for yourself for achieving those goals.

2. What goals did you set last year that you didn't achieve? Let's apply a growth mindset to these. What happened that had you miss the mark and what can we learn as we move ahead with this year's goals?

3. What are some juicy stretch goals for you this year that would also feel kind and compassionate in the broader context of your life? What kind goals do you want to set?

4. Use the scorecard I created for you here to ensure these goals are supportive and aligned with your purposeful ambition.

· KIND GOAL SETTING

	GOAL 1	GOAL 2	GOAL 3
IS IT PSYCHOLOGICALLY SAFE?			
AM I MOVING AT THE SPEED OF TRUST?			
IS IT A STRETCH GOAL?			
AM I CONNECTED TO MY PURPOSE?			
AM I LEVERAGING MY UNIQUE GIFTS?			
AM I HONORING MY NEEDS?			
IS MY MINDSET EXPANSIVE?			
DOES THIS HONOR MY CONTENTMENT?			

CREATING HEALTHY HABITS

The best way to honor a goal is to turn it into a healthy ambitious habit. Habits are essential to accomplishing our aims. They instigate change gradually, guiding us to weave and ritualize actions into our daily life, significantly enhancing the likelihood of achieving your goal.

James Clear, author of the bestselling *Atomic Habits*, has a few techniques we can use to ensure our habits stick so we can reach our objectives. Let's explore them together.

Set a Cue

Cues are catalysts that initiate a habitual behavior. To set cues, we want to make sure they are unmissable. When I first started a habit of working with my mindset reframes every day, I needed a visible cue to remind me to do it. At home, I have a little meditation cushion set up in the corner of my bedroom next to my red light. Initially when I began working with my mindset reframes, I placed a set of index cards on top of my meditation cushion as a visual cue to remind me to work with them every day after my meditation. You can do something similar. Let's say you want to journal every morning. You might create a cue for yourself by placing your journal next to your bed so it's the first thing you encounter when you wake up.

Remove Friction

In order to use cues more consistently, we need to remove as much friction as possible. A few years into the pandemic, my client Noah got really tired of cooking, a habit she picked up when the virus spread rapidly around New York City and restaurants shuttered. As someone who had a background in fitness, she was conscientious about cooking meals that were great for her family's health. But after twelve months of readying three meals a day, she was exhausted by the effort required and stopped cooking. Noah realized that if she wanted to maintain the habit of feeding her family healthy and nutritious meals, she needed to remove the friction of the prep work. So she signed up for a meal delivery service that provides vegetables and proteins you can mix and match to make your own meals. In doing so, she removed all the preparation time from her weekly cooking but still got to eat things she and her family loved. (P.S. She was able to do that because she had the money. Money can remove a lot of friction, and that's one reason I'm an advocate for you having more of it.)

Start Temptation Bundling

Another suggestion Clear offers, and which I've leveraged with my clients, is to use "temptation bundling." Temptation bundling uses dopamine, the neurotransmitter responsible for motivation, to our advantage by syncing up a habit we love to do with one that we don't yet quite enjoy. So if you're passionate about going outside to get your daily dose of vitamin D and support your circadian rhythms, but you can't yet commit to daily meditation, sync the two. Go outside to get your sun, which you love, and do a walking meditation that you can listen to on your cell phone.

Celebrate Your Wins

Making our habits feel celebratory also helps us stick to them. As motivated, high-achieving folks, we've often got our eyes on the next milestone and forget to pause and reward ourselves for everything we've done to get here. But it helps, especially when our goals require delayed gratification. Because outcomes are often beyond our control, I often invite my clients to celebrate the habits and actions they took *toward* their goals, not just when they reach their goals.

When I was working with Leila and her $600,000 year, we celebrated every week that she took consistent action. Sometimes she'd reward herself with fancy nail art, sometimes with putting a hundred dollars in her travel fund, and sometimes with a nice dinner with friends. The celebrations were like a cherry on top of the habit and gave her the motivation to keep at it. Not celebrating our wins takes us out of contentment because we're so future-focused, which can cause us to inadvertently occupy our painful ambition.

You can celebrate by:

- Taking yourself out for a nice date to a museum, concert, or great dinner

- Buying yourself flowers

- Making or buying yourself a celebration cake, complete with candles to blow out

- Hosting a celebration circle with your closest friends, where each person shares what they're celebrating about you

Go One Step at a Time

Another way to create habits you stick to is to go step-by-step. As humans, we often make things more complicated than they need to be. When we think about our stretch goal, we often think of the hundred steps we need to take instead of just focusing on the first one. Many of us fail to begin because we're focused so far down the path, we forget that we can start where we are.

This reminds me of the TV show *Unbreakable Kimmy Schmidt*. Early in season one of this satirical series, we learn that Kimmy was in captivity at Reverend Richard Wayne Gary Wayne's bunker, home of his "Spooky Church of the Scary-pocalypse." In one episode, Kimmy flashes back to the days in the bunker where the reverend would have her and her other captors turn a mystery crank twenty-four hours a day. In one of the first episodes, Kimmy explains how she's able to keep moving the crank. "See, you can stand anything for ten seconds. Then, you just start on a new ten seconds. . . . So, whether you're turning a heavy crank, the purpose of which is unknown to this day, or just waiting around to open some presents, all you gotta do is take it ten seconds at a time."[4]

In the show, the crank is a metaphor for the endurance and misogyny women are made to withstand on a daily basis, but Kimmy has made another great point: We can do anything for just about ten seconds a day. Gay Hendricks says that to start honoring our zone of genius, we need only start with ten minutes a day. Kimmy says start with ten seconds. Regardless, the lesson is to start small and work your way up from there.

Honor Your Energy

I often think how different the world of work would be if we allowed people to design their jobs (and their habits) around their unique energy. We all have different brains and bodies, which means we are not all designed to work in the same ways and at the same pace. And when we force ourselves to do that, we often end up dropping the ball, or hurting ourselves, because we're *fighting* our energy instead of *flowing* with it.

Let's take women and people with a uterus, for example. Many of us who produce estrogen have an infradian rhythm known as the menstrual cycle. And though the menstrual cycle typically lasts twenty-three to thirty-five days, hormones in the menstrual cycle shift every single day. What that means is those of us navigating this cycle have different energy levels, moods, and bodily feedback every day. It confounds me that we are expected to produce and contribute the same way each day when biologically and hormonally this is impossible.

Let's say, for example, you have committed to strength training five days a week but in the luteal phase of your cycle (the phase leading up to your period), you are so exhausted that strength training would do more harm than good. In this case, we want to adjust for that—instead of strength training, you go for a nice walk or take a yoga class. This is not you making excuses; this is honoring your body and your goals at the very same time. If we have to manipulate our bodies in impossible ways to achieve a desired outcome, that, my friends, is classic painful ambition.

So, what does this look like at work? As someone who has two chronic illnesses, I need to be tuned in to when my body functions optimally and when it needs a big ol' nap to run my business effectively. I also know I do my best thinking work early in the week and first thing in the morning. So Mondays are usually my CEO days where I do strategic and visionary work, like designing curricula or writing articles. When I was writing this book, I would write on Mondays and Tuesdays, starting early in the day. When my brain has done a lot of focused work it tends to slow down by four o'clock, so that is when I would reply to my emails. Wednesday and Thursday were reserved for coaching work, and by Friday my brain was pretty spent, so that was when I would do any light-lift or spillover work. Usually that looked like listening to edits of my podcast, catching up on emails, and organizing documents for my bookkeeper. If I forced myself to write every single day, I wouldn't get it done because my brain needs a break to pause and process.

You might be the sort of person who has the best and most creative ideas once the sun goes down. Great! Design your work around that. Or perhaps you're an early riser and love to get the intensive parts of your job done before the rest of the world wakes. Awesome! Design around that.

Whenever I share this idea in workshops, someone's hand inevitably shoots up, and they'll disclose that it feels impossible to set new habits with this level of agility when so much of their life is governed by a corporate schedule. While it is more challenging because you're working inside of an existing structure, it's not impossible. In fact, I have many clients who build freedom in the framework of corporate work. The trick is to focus on the parts of your schedule you do have agency over and design your habits in those pockets. For example, I once coached a man named Liam who was the head of sales for a global TV network. He managed a large team and felt he had little control over his schedule as a result. But when we looked at his calendar together, we saw most of his direct reports met with him in the afternoon. We consolidated his one-on-ones to Monday and Tuesday afternoons, then blocked his calendar for the mornings so he could do his strategic work then. Though not every week could be the same because he traveled often, he had a plan for 80 percent of his time that made his work feel a lot more fulfilling.

Stay Accountable

Lastly, when it comes to creating a healthy ambitious habit, accountability is key. Whether you are staying accountable to yourself via a tracking system or checking in with a friend or coach, being held accountable goes a long way to achieving your goals. Remember, stretch goals need to be both psychologically safe *and* have accountability around them. Use the trackers below to support your follow-through with your habits.

TRACKING YOUR HEALTHY
AMBITIOUS HABITS

	MON	TUES	WED	THURS	FRI	SAT	SUN
HABIT 1							
HABIT 2							
HABIT 3							
HABIT 4							
HABIT 5							
HABIT 6							

WEEKLY HEALTHY
AMBITIOUS HABITS CHECK-IN

	HABIT 1	HABIT 2	HABIT 3
DID I HONOR THIS HABIT?			
DID I REMOVE FRICTION?			
DID I MAKE IT BITE-SIZE?			
DID ANYTHING GET IN THE WAY?			
WHAT CAN I DO TO MAKE THIS MORE SEAMLESS?			
HOW WILL I CELEBRATE TAKING ACTION?			

MAKING FRIENDS WITH FEAR

A few years ago I was helping my client Imani slowly step away from her accounting career and into the world of public speaking. Though she was a CPA, she had a natural talent for communications and wanted to further explore that area. We decided that a low-stakes way to follow her curiosity without quitting her day job was to get curious about starting an informal speaking tour. Imani loved connecting with others, having deep and meaningful conversations, and saying the things that others were afraid to say. Free-flowing public speaking was a gift of hers, so this made perfect sense as a vehicle to explore. As we positioned the series, we built the story around her lived experience as a Black, American, corporate tax accountant who was exploring why achieving everything she thought she wanted had made her so profoundly discontented.

As we contemplated what a minimal viable launch could look like, we built out the brand story, the visuals, her signature talks, and her dream stages. Then, when Imani was set to reach out to book her talks, the crippling fear took over. Though we were three months into the process, all of a sudden she was worried about what her mother and friends would say. She started to convince herself this was a terrible idea and that she didn't even like speaking to people. She became terrified that putting herself out there in such a public way would make her a target. I listened and lovingly held space for her as each fear came up. Imani enjoyed sharing her ideas and her voice; she was so excited about this idea. But the more fear took center stage, the more it eclipsed the excitement she had initially felt.

Have you ever seen *Indiana Jones and the Last Crusade*? In

this epic movie from Harrison Ford's heyday, there is an iconic scene where, in order to save his dad's life, Jones has to take a leap of faith and walk across a chasm that has no footbridge. He's at the edge of a craggy cliff, needing to make it to the other side to save his dad from the peril that is to come. He glances down to see nothing but a steep, cavernous drop that seems to have no bottom. He contemplates what to do. He's terrified and knows he can't make the jump across the divide. Then he hears his dad screaming in pain, and he realizes he has no choice but to take a step forward. As he readies himself, he has an epiphany. "It's a leap of faith," he whispers. Jones takes a deep breath and then kicks his leg out to take the first step, half expecting to fall to his death. And you know what happens? As he moves forward into what should have been a catastrophic fall into the abyss, a footbridge catches him. He stumbles in surprise. It was an optical illusion—the way was always there.[5]

In many ways, leaving the old and familiar to step into the new and more aligned can feel like a daunting leap of faith. But more often than not, the path forward is already there. When I help clients navigate the shift from a career chosen through painful ambition to a more purposeful profession, inevitably fear arises. It usually comes at the moment when we have already done most of the work, have named and claimed the direction we're headed in, and are ready to put our stake into the ground of something new. Almost like clockwork, the voice of fear and discomfort comes knocking. *Do you really want to do that thing you're about to do?* it says. *Do you feel worthy? Maybe you* don't *have the skills* and *The timing* isn't *right.* All our voices of fear sound a little different, but they are designed to do the same thing: keep us stuck in our comfort zone.

Remember when I referred to subconscious sabotage as safety restoration? That's because sometimes it is. When it comes to claiming our ambitious next level, fear raises its little head because our brains are hardwired to keep us safe, and growth can feel terrifying. Recent studies have even shown that feeling emotional pain is akin to feeling physical pain. In fact, through the use of functional brain MRIs, one study found that the emotional sensation of rejection lights up centers of the brain responsible for physical distress.[6] In other words, fear can actually feel like a deep ache in our bodies. It's no wonder we create protective barriers to keep us in the cozy comfort zone.

Our fear isn't the full story. That little, protective voice of fear, if we listen to it, is keeping us from our wildest dreams. In fact, most of our most challenging emotions are an expression of our fear. When we feel jealous that someone has done something we want to do, it's our fear saying we can't do it. When our anxiety is saying everything will go wrong, it's our fear saying we're going to be harmed. When we think we're being practical or realistic, it's our fear talking us out of our dreams. The truth is, we're all afraid. That is completely natural. But being afraid doesn't mean we can't still embody our courage. In fact, being afraid often means we are inching toward our bravest parts.

That said, fear can be useful because it is information. It points to an emotion that needs expressing or a need that requires addressing. Fear can masquerade as laziness, anger, anxiety, and even depression.[7] The objective isn't to be so courageous that we never feel fear (I don't know any humans like that), but to feel the fear, understand what it's signaling to us, identify what is a true threat and what is a distortion, and move ahead anyway. Fear is meant to tell us when we are in danger. But most of us are not being chased by grizzly bears in the wild. We are being chased by fear-based thoughts that are often not fact-based. Of course all feelings are valid, whether they are fact-based or not. But separating fact and fiction can help us take steps toward the life we really want versus allowing ourselves to stay frozen in our fear story.

Our fears can feel even more amplified if we've experienced trauma because, as we learned in chapter 2, trauma impacts our beliefs and experiences. In fact, studies suggest that children who have experienced trauma often have brains that are wired for fear.[8] While trauma is prevalent, and almost three quarters of us will experience one traumatic event in our lifetime, the most marginalized are at the most risk: youth of color tend to experience more trauma than their white counterparts, queer youths tend to have more adverse childhood events than their heterosexual peers, women are more likely to experience PTSD than men, and those with disabilities are more likely to experience abuse.[9] As historically excluded people, it's not always just about mindset-shifting our way out of fear because we are often having a full-body response. And those full-body responses are typically connected to our trauma and can hinder our ability to move forward.

In the famed book about the mind-body connection, *The Body Keeps the Score: Brain, Mind, and Body in the Healing of Trauma*, author Bessel van der Kolk, MD, writes, "The only way we can change the way we feel is by becoming aware of our inner experience and learning to befriend what is going on inside ourselves."[10] (Note: van der Kolk has recently come under scrutiny for his problematic treatment of employees and for falsifying data. But this idea is reinforced across many different bodies of research.) If we try to push down fear, override it with action, or explain it away, it likely won't work because the trauma is stored in our body, and we cannot deny its existence or impact.

When Imani started to share with me all of her fears around launching the speaking series, the first place we looked was mindset. But what quickly became apparent was that there was trauma there. Her parents had become very successful and publicly visible in their hometown with several restaurant locations, and then, due to unforeseen circumstances, had lost everything. As a result, she was afraid to step into her bigness and take up space. This trauma was stored in her body, and every time she thought of getting on-stage, she felt the very same feelings she felt when she witnessed her parents lose what they had spent decades building. When clients have experienced trauma and it's getting in the way of what they really desire for their lives, I often recommend a therapeutic intervention such as EMDR or somatic work. If the pain is stored in our bodies, no amount of mindset work will shift us. And that is what Imani went on to do.

Most of what we desire for our next level of growth is something we've never experienced before. And novel experiences can feel unsafe for our bodies. Since our nervous systems are largely responsible for what we feel and how we behave, we need to make sure they feel safe to progress. Though I have been trained in trauma-informed coaching, I am not a therapist, so when my clients uncover or point to traumatic experiences, I often recommend parallel-path coaching with trauma therapies. Certain practices can help us manage the symptoms of trauma and how we navigate those feelings and sensations in the moment. Over time they can give us the tools we need to move forward. But anytime someone is having challenges moving forward, it's never because they can't do hard things; more likely it's because hard things have happened to them and are stored in their bodies and brains. When ambitious humans can't move ahead it's not because they lack the aptitude— it's usually because trauma has wedged its way into our cells and our bodies feel as though we're unsafe.

Managing Our Mental Filters

Sometimes when our fear becomes too great, we start to use mental filters or cognitive distortions that amplify the negative and turn the volume down on the positive.

For example, the reality is, we are living in fear-inducing times and a lot these fears are really legitimate. However, we want to see if we might be living in a distortion in certain areas and if we can release any fears to make our lived experience a little less anxiety-inducing. Here are the common mental filters defined by cognitive behavioral therapy practices:

> *Catastrophizing.* You automatically assume the absolute worst outcome will happen. For example, catastrophic thinking tells you that if you don't hear back from the recruiter about the job you want in a timely fashion, it's because they hated you and you'll never get a job ever again. This is very common, particularly in challenging economic and political times like the ones we're living in. But it also feeds irrational fears. If we look at history, yes, worst-case scenarios can come true, but they are usually a rarity.

> *Overgeneralizing.* This skews our lens of reality because we believe that if something happened once, it will certainly happen again. In this filter, the beliefs don't have to be personal. Something we've witnessed on the news

or know about via other people can also reinforce these beliefs. For example, you think that every time you present to the CEO he's going to pick holes in your presentation. You've seen it happen to your colleagues so it must always be true.

Superstition. This is where we think something bad might happen if we make a certain choice, even if it is completely unrelated to the situation at hand. Superstitions can be perpetuated by cultural ideologies and also feed irrational fears and anxiety. For example, if you don't knock on wood when someone says you'll surely get a promotion, you think it's not going to happen for you.

Sometimes, we might not even know we have a mental filter until someone else points it out to us. Growing up Arab and raised Muslim, I absorbed some pretty strong ideas around the evil eye. In our home, we believed that people's feelings of jealousy could actually cause us harm or misfortune. In fact, my dad thought that my sister's juvenile diabetes diagnosis was a result of the evil eye— despite the fact that he was a physician. He would regularly tell my sisters and me to hide our thick hair by "making a ponytail" so people wouldn't be jealous and cast their evil eye upon us. So deep did this belief run that when I got into a car crash at the age of seventeen, my very first thought was, *Thank God I'm alive*, followed by, *It must have been someone's evil eye* (not the fact that I was fiddling with Mariah Carey CDs and not paying attention to the road).

I carried this belief everywhere. I would wear nice clothes, but nothing too nice, because people might put their evil eye on me. I would share my achievements, but not the biggest ones because people might cause me harm with their evil eye. Superstition is a through line of many cultures and can have us living in a distortion. And because superstitions are reinforced by our families and society, they can be hard to release.

Years ago, when I first worked with a mindset coach, I told her all about the evil eye and how it either had ruined or had potential to ruin my life. I'll never forget her face—she looked like a deer in headlights. I could tell I was the first person to introduce her to the idea of a jinn. I told her story after story of when someone's evil eye had caused me harm, from my car accident and autoimmune diagnosis, to losing my favorite necklace, to my hair falling out. She listened patiently and respectfully, and then rather dryly said, "You know that is entirely superstitious, right?" Then she asked, "What are some other plausible explanations for these events that don't have to do with evil entities?"

In one session, I started to see that maybe people weren't out to get me. Just maybe I shouldn't have been shuffling Mariah's *Butterfly* album while driving! Perhaps my genes, my environment, and my beliefs were more to do with my illnesses than an evil eye. My necklace was old and had a lot of wear and tear. And everyone knows hair loss is a symptom of Hashimoto's. But until she reflected these ideas back to me, I lived in fear of the evil eye, and it felt very real to me.

Maybe you, like me, have lived according to a superstition, or have felt like Imani and pumped the brakes just before the finish line. All of us have had times in our lives when we've let fear or mental filters run the show and get in the way of our ambitious life. To begin letting go, we start by identifying the ways your fear stories may be intercepting the life you want.

Exercise:
Identify Your Fear Stories

1. Ask yourself, "When it comes to my next level of expression, what am I afraid of right now?" Make a list, write the story, jot down all the reasons you feel fearful. Don't leave anything off the page. This is your space to put it all out there without judgment.

2. Check in and see where you might be using a mental filter like catastrophizing, overgeneralizing, or being superstitious.

3. For all the fears you listed, I want you to separate them into three columns: most likely not going to happen, low to medium chance of happening, high chance of happening.

4. For the fears that may have a high chance of happening, we want to put together a game plan to mitigate that outcome. What can we do to lessen the impact or to have a backup plan in place for the worst-case scenario? Choose the fear that is most alive for you and answer the three questions below:

   * What can I do to prevent it?
   * What can I do to lessen its impact?
   * What is my plan for the worst-case scenario?

5. We can stay out of our stories by having integrity with our actions. What actions will you take to keep yourself out of fear and cognitive distortions and move into integrity?

6. Make a list of your strengths and where you are the most courageous, inviting your brain to believe in your own resilience and fortitude—even in the hardest moments. This exercise serves as a reminder that even in the most difficult moments, you are capable. Read this list every day (along with your list of gifts!).

CREATING INTERNAL STABILITY

Much of the time when I'm working with clients on their career, purpose, or an ambitious pivot, it can feel really scary to make big changes, for financial reasons and even personal safety. There are very real consequences women (and other historically excluded people) face that often impact our ability to grow. In fact, studies have shown that women are much more likely to face negative consequences of their risk-taking, while men faced much more positive outcomes.[11] So how do we feel the fear and do it anyway?

When we're coming from a place of wholeness and we want to do something big, we need to cultivate internal stability and bring in the "unbothered energy" in order to do so. Unbothered energy is when we know who we are so deeply and have created enough internal stability that when unfavorable things happen on the outside, our sense of self is unshaken. You want to occupy the fullness of your gifts and bring forth the best that is within you in any given moment, right? That takes something. It reminds me of one of my favorite quotes from *The Velveteen Rabbit*. The rabbit asks the skin horse what it means to be real. The skin horse replies in a way that moved me so much:

> It takes a long time. That's why it doesn't often happen to people who break easily, or have sharp edges, or who have to be carefully kept. Generally, by the time you are Real, most of your hair has been loved off, and your eyes drop out and you get loose in the joints and very shabby. But these things don't matter at all, because once you are Real you can't be ugly, except to people who don't understand.[12]

Something happens when we become real, when we align with a more whole version of our ambition and we swap our performance-filled life for purpose. Friendships transform, people fall away, but those who remain are the ones who can see and support your greatness. Many of my clients fear this moment, and it's often something that holds them back from their growth. But those who fall away are a small loss compared to what and who is gained. The ones who don't join us on the journey are the ones who think our growth is ugly. In my view, nothing is more beautiful than our humanity unfolding. And so, let's send those people love and send them on their way.

Many of us stall our growth because we're afraid of failing and being judged. But the truth is, we'll be judged regardless. We're worried about what our parents or strangers on the internet are going to say. But you could be perfectly demure, voiceless, and in a corner *and still be judged*, so you may as well be yourself. Others' judgment of you has to do with them and where they feel unexpressed—that is their material. That's their projection. When you feel more impervious to the opinions others hold of you, you will experience far less suffering. Of course that's a challenging thing to do, and we are all works in progress trying to figure out how to do that for ourselves. But like I said, whether you take up space or not, people are going to have an opinion about it. So you might as well be the you-est you. Be the main character of your own life. Main characters show up in main character energy regardless of the room or circumstance. You are your biggest source of stability. The world around us will always introduce obstacles—that is the nature of life. But if your internal foundation is solid, you will have the power to do the extraordinary. And your unwavering devotion to be your rooted, brilliant self will light the way for others.

Exercise:
Cultivate Main Character
Energy and Stability

1. In your notebook, make two columns. At the top of column one, write "self." At the top of column two, write "not self."

2. In the "self" column, list out all the attributes you are at your core. Who did you come to planet earth as before the world projected ideas onto you? Think of your perfect little childhood self. What qualities did they unabashedly embody?

3. In the "not self" column, list out all the ways you are your fearful, anxiety-driven, judgmental, and painful self.

4. Over the next week, notice where and when you are living in self versus not self energy.

5. When you notice yourself in not self energy, use the body mapping tool in chapter 6 to regulate your nervous system and bring you back to self energy. Practice this until it becomes your default. This is how we create internal stability.

⋘⋙

Remember this: fear and hurdles will always be present. But our response should never be to renounce our ambition or fail to take aligned action because we dread the repercussions—it's to create internal stability for ourselves, then call on our communities and rally our allies as we march confidently forward toward the beautiful lives we deserve.

Chapter Summary

- When it comes to taking aligned action, your goals should be both kind and psychologically safe.

- Create healthy habits for yourself through setting cues, temptation bundling, and removing friction.

- Go step-by-step, and honor your unique energy.

- Fear will always be there—especially when taking big actions. Use the fear-stories exercise to make friends with fear.

- You are the main character of your life—live like it.

- Create internal stability for yourself by working with your nervous system.

CONCLUSION

As you go out into the world ready to contribute your brilliance in an even bigger way, I want you to remember this: ambition is yours for the taking. It will look different from what you've seen out in the world because much of what we've been shown is largely dysfunctional and even harmful, especially for those of us who come from marginalized communities. If your ambitious ideas look different from the norm, that's great news—they need to. I want to invite you to leverage your purposeful ambition for something really revolutionary. After all, if we're going to dismantle racism, the patriarchy, and ableism, and heal from late-stage capitalism, our purposeful contributions need to be profound.

After reading this book, your goals may have shifted, or perhaps the why behind them has. Maybe you cracked open this book looking for insights on how to get a promotion because you wanted to be the first person with your identity to make it to partner at your firm, but as you moved from chapter to chapter, you realized that's not actually your dream. Or perhaps you thumbed through the pages looking for ways to own more of your power at work, only to realize entrepreneurship is the way you can have the biggest impact. When it comes to reimagining our lives and choosing goals that align with our healthy ambitions, you don't have to push or force anything. Your journey is about choosing the aligned action every day that brings you closer to what feels true for you.

You have so much talent, fire, and brilliance within you. You stand on the shoulders of all your ancestors, mentors, and people that have loved you. Yes, each of us who is doing this work has known struggle, perhaps more struggle than most. But let's not let it be in vain. I want you to use any resistance as fuel, as fire, and as an opening to create a radically different world.

As we bring our journey to a close, I want you to keep your vision high and remember a few important ideas as you get on the court with your purposeful ambition.

KEEP UNFOLDING

One of the hardest moments in my career happened a few years ago while I was also writing this book. I was trucking along with my usual business model when all of a sudden, out of nowhere, things just broke. My tried-and-true tactics were yielding nada. I kicked and screamed a little bit, revisited all my frameworks, and spoke to therapists, coaches, and friends alike. And you know what they all said to me? *Amina, you're playing too small. You've been here and done this. What's next? It's time to claim that.*

From the outside, that didn't look entirely true. I had made decently bold moves and thrown my hat in the ring for things. I have a book deal with one of the world's major publishers, for Pete's sake! But upon closer inspection, they were absolutely freaking right. I had achieved many of the things I had set out to do. But in reality, I was resting on my laurels and calling it contentment when I knew, deep down, there was a desire to continue to unfold. In my efforts to avoid becoming an ambition monster, I had become something almost as ill-fitting: complacent.

Let this be your reminder to keep unfolding. Sometimes we arrive at a place that we have deeply desired to go, and we stop so long to enjoy the view we forget to check back in with that internal voice that says *I have more to contribute*. And because it's already so radical that we underrecognized people have gotten this far, sometimes we trick ourselves into believing it's enough. Or maybe we think tapping into our growth is a one-and-done activity. As long as you have breath in your lungs, you are meant to keep unfolding. Give yourself permission to keep journeying toward your constellation of purpose each and every day. Allow yourself to be the brightest, shiniest person in the room. Keep letting your soul speak.

If you were to give your soul a voice and let it direct your next level of purposeful ambition, what would it say?

SURRENDER YOUR GROWTH

Now that we've stretched a little more, we're going to—wait for it—completely surrender our vision. You may be thinking, *WHAT? Amina, I'm a doer, a high achiever, a make-things-happen kind of person. I don't surrender!*

I see you, I feel you, I *was* you.

A lot of us use our goals as a vehicle to control our lives. But there is an element of faith and surrender, a quiet receptivity, that is required for us to achieve that next level. Surrender isn't waving the white flag or giving up; it's the absence of resistance. Surrender is not about stopping the action. It's a mindset shift into full faith in a higher power while also showing up in the action. It's the idea that we can take all the aligned steps, and things may still turn out differently than we desired. That is okay—that is life and that is information. When we stop fighting for control and start flowing instead, our experience of life is vastly different. The magic happens in the fluidity between both passive and exerted energy. An excess of one and not enough of the other throws our efforts out of balance. Too much passive energy can make us idle, while too much exerted energy can make us destructive. Finding that harmony, in and of itself, is pretty darn radical.

It's worth noting that sometimes the idea of surrender is used in spiritual communities in a way that stymies our critical thinking— it's a form of spiritual bypass. We've likely all been part of a conversation where we were told to "give it over to God," or the universe, in a way that felt like it took our power and our agency away. What I'm saying is distinct from that. We want to be both surrendered to the outcome but using our own inner wisdom and agency every step of the way.

LEAN INTO FAITH

Once we have surrendered to what will be, faith becomes the highest-yield place for us to rest. When I say the word "faith," people often have an allergic reaction to it. But I don't mean faith in a specific religious context. I'm not a religious person. I was raised in a Muslim household, but as I grew up, I realized my relationship to the divine was deeply personal. In my opinion, faith isn't about a specific religion but about leaning into the knowledge that a higher power has your back and is always working to support you. Faith asks us to accept something not on the basis of reason but on the basis of trust.

To trust in the energy that makes flowers grow, that causes the earth to spin on its axis, and that brought us to the planet is faith. Faith is a very visionary idea to believe in. Faith is trusting that a higher power knows what it's doing with us and for us. Even when things feel like they're going sideways. Our attempt to control that energy only impedes it. Without faith we are aimlessly forcing what isn't ours to force.

Faith hasn't always been an easy place for me to land. Shortly after my initial health scare, I felt very angry with God, the universe, a higher power—however you refer to it. I'd navigated so many hard things that I thought surely the universe had forgotten me or was far too busy to support me. (Can you relate?) But telling myself the story that I was on my own was only further perpetuating the difficult feelings.

One day, I sat down with my coach, who was a former Vaishnava monk, and lamented over the challenge of the day. I went on for about ten minutes and he just let me speak and ramble. Once I was done, he paused for what felt like an eternity and asked me, "What if *that* was God?" He went on to ask, "What if every challenge you've had in your life, and the fact that you've gotten through them all, is God?" He took one more long pause and then said, "The challenge is *also* the gift from the divine."

I thought about it for a long while. I journaled on it. I meditated on it. I talked through it, and I realized he was right. If I didn't have the upbringing I had, I wouldn't have shown up in the world the way I did. If I didn't show up in the world the way I did, I wouldn't have almost worked myself into an early grave. If I hadn't almost died, I wouldn't have sought out tools to change my life. If I hadn't sought out tools to change my life, I wouldn't have become a coach. If I hadn't become a coach, I wouldn't be writing this book or teaching seminars or training leaders. The challenge has been the gift.

Listen, do I sometimes wish life was less challenging? Of course I do. I know you do, too. And at the same time, I know deep in my soul that the biggest challenges have made way for the deepest teachings, and I would never shortchange them. To this day, whenever I find myself in uncomfortable and taxing scenarios, I ask myself, *What if this is God?* I recognize this can sound like toxic positivity—the idea that everything, no matter how terrible, is somehow serving us. Some stuff just sucks and has no rhyme or reason. But what I know for me is that it is much more supportive to rest in the idea that God looks out for me and that there is some good in all this than it is to believe that I have been abandoned. Welcome all the feelings *and* lean into faith.

Even, or perhaps most especially, welcome grief.

On November 4, 2018, my maternal grandfather, whom I viewed as my father figure, passed away. He had prostate cancer that had metastasized up and down his body, and, in the last few weeks, to his brain. To say that I loved this person is the understatement of the century. He was grounded, unbelievably kind, witty, loved me and my sisters unconditionally, and was my stability in this world. The home he shared with my grandmother was the only real home we knew, having moved over a dozen times as children.

It didn't matter what happened—he always had my back. He was God in human form to me. When he died, I lost my mind for a bit. I was devastated. I think it was six months before I was able to stop the daily tears. Every day I felt a deep ache in my heart. I felt it so much and so often, I decided it was time to get to know this feeling that was living in me like a parasite. I met my grief so deeply that it became an entire body of work.

Grief is universal, and we experience it everywhere if we'll allow it. There is grief in leaving a job, moving to a new city, losing a loved one, being outbid on your dream home, having entrepreneurship unfold much differently that you thought it would. Grief is everywhere. And if I hadn't met it so deeply, I couldn't teach it. Grief, for me, was a portal in getting closer to God and getting closer to my work. Resting in the idea that one of the hardest moments of my life was actually one of my most profound openings is how I now see faith.

CULTIVATE DEVOTION

In the spiritual lineages that I have studied under, there is a lot of talk about devotion. Devotion to the work, devotion to change, devotion to healing, devotion to our practices. When I explored the origins of the word "devotion" something crystalized for me. Devotion comes from the Latin word *devovere* meaning consecrate, which means to dedicate to a divine purpose.[1] How beautiful is that? As we wrap up our work together, I want to ask you: What will you be devoted to as you move forward?

A lot of the entrepreneurial and career-related organizations I've been a part of have spoken endlessly of discipline. We hear stories of "hacking" our discipline, and how the most disciplined of us are the ones that "win." Discipline is taught as the gold standard. And if we look up its definition we learn it's "the practice of training people to obey rules or a code of behavior," which for me has always felt in violation of my true nature. What if instead of disciplining ourselves to observe a set of rules and behaviors, we allowed ourselves to be disciples (which has the same root word), meaning students. How about, instead of strong-arming ourselves to follow a set of codes that were likely not designed to support people like us, we committed to being students dedicated to our divine purpose? To be a disciple or student, in my opinion, is one of the most beautiful roles we could take on because it asks us *What are we devoted to?* And if all of us devoted our lives to expressing divine purpose, what a beautiful world it would be.

Let's harness our devotion together. We must be more devoted to our world-changing mission than we are to our doubts. We must be more devoted to our faith than we are to our limiting beliefs. We must be more devoted to helping ourselves and others than we are to our pain. We must be more devoted to our healing than we are to the systems that have harmed us and the trauma they have caused. Let your devotion light the way.

What I want for you, more than anything, is for you to leverage your purposeful ambition in service of the life you desire. What this world needs more than ever is people who look like us and identify as we do, redefining what it means to embody power in a way that serves all people and the planet. As a historically excluded person, being aligned and living with purpose is an act of resistance and creates a next-level transformation for our world. When we are in the right relationship with ambition, success, and our purpose, we are doing more than just aligning with our soul's calling. We are honoring our lineage, healing broken systems, and shifting culture.

We have the tools we need and are equipped to meet this unjust world head on, propelled by our dreams. If we want to experience a different reality, we have to choose a different way. That means showing up in all the work we've done so far and swinging for something really game-changing.

This book was designed to level up your way of being and, by virtue of that, enhance all the parts of your work and life. There's often a moment in each of our lives where we feel like we've hit a ceiling—like we've done all we can with the tools that we have and we just can't seem to arrive at that next level of becoming. Here's the truth: we can't arrive at a different outcome with the same old beliefs, thoughts, and methods that got us where we are. It requires a paradigm shift—which we have laid the groundwork for in this book. When it comes to our growth, I believe that there are seasons we need to grow incrementally, and there are seasons we get to leap into radical growth. And if you are ready to put all of this work into practice, I want to invite you into that conversation of radical growth.

The beauty of radical growth is that it requires us to put ourselves out there for all the things we thought were for anybody but us. It's to ask for the radical raise or radical promotion, to apply for the job that feels like a radical shift, to move to the new city that would bring radical happiness, to radically shift our relationships, to take a radical rest, etc. Radical growth changes the game.

GO GET YOUR DREAMS

You are worthy of everything you want in this world even though society (and sometimes our own mindset) has perpetually reinforced that you're not. I hope now, by the end of this book, you can see what a steaming pile of garbage that is. If the vision lies within you, it is for you. Yes, some of us may face more headwinds than others, but the dream is there for us. And the more we take courageous action toward it, the more we invite others that look and identify like we do to do the same. The more empowered historically excluded people we have in the world, the less oppression there will be. The less oppression there is, the more peace is possible. It's our time to shine, my friends. This moment has been a long time in the making, and I plan to seize it with all of you.

The only trap would be believing that our ambitious dreams are not possible for us. And I refuse to let any of us fall into that.

ACKNOWLEDGMENTS

Writing a book is a portal to a new and different version of yourself. I could never, in a million years, have transcended the threshold without the amazing group of humans who ushered me through. It would be nearly impossible to list all the people who brought this work to life, so I will also say a heartfelt thank-you to every teacher, community group, mentor, colleague, and friend who has shaped me and this work. I offer a deep and reverent bow to you all.

To every single one of my clients: I love you. Thank you for saying yes to your own transformation and big, beautiful life. Thank you for trusting me with your growth—it's the greatest privilege to sit beside you as you bravely and magnificently choose yourself. There's no bigger nor more courageous work than that.

To you, dear reader. Bless you for getting this far. Thank you for picking up this book—that itself is an act of valor and a way to unabashedly bet on your dreams. May this work be of the highest service to you.

To Nitika, my best friend, cheerleader, and fierce *pataki*. Thank you for endlessly listening as I sifted through the beauty and the pain. Thank you for helping me carry the weight when it was too heavy on my own. Thank you for teaching us all how to move through the tough stuff to get to the good stuff. God really broke the mold with you, and I pray everyone finds a soul sister with no sense, no chill, no shame.

Ericka and Stephanie, thank you from the bottom of my heart for SEEING ME and this work and knowing there was something here. Thank you for lending your brilliance to this project and making it into what it is. Ericka, your Capricorn genius and profound clarity were exactly the big-sister, get-shit-done energy I needed. I am forever grateful for who you are in this world and who you have been to me. We should do this again sometime. 😜

Porochista, you were a *fierce* guardian of the work. Thank you for holding me and the book in integrity. Your eye, your gift of the written word, and your love of the world made this project the nuanced body of work it is. Bless you for being, and for being on this journey with me.

Nina, what can I say? Two minutes into our meeting I knew I wanted my book to go to you. You are wisdom and grace personified and are changing the industry, one book and author at a time. It's the honor of a lifetime that you said yes to *The Ambition Trap.* What a gift it was to lean into you and your guidance. Thank you for helping me KonMari the book and for being the literary doula of my dreams!

To the rest of the PRH team, whom I know worked tirelessly to support this book: Brian, Meg, Shelby, Alex, and Bridget. Bless you for saying yes and dedicating time, energy, and effort to making this work shine.

To my publicity team, Jessie and Sarah, who remind me to show up and shine every day. Thank you.

To Cams and Sam for holding down the fort and simultaneously buoying me up. You two are angels.

ACKNOWLEDGMENTS

Pilar, thank you for holding the vision for the brand and this beautiful cover. Thank you for your brilliant eye and for knowing how to translate me so seamlessly.

Deganit, there are some people who are the grand weavers of our lives—and you are one of those people for me. If you hadn't introduced me to Stacey, and Stacey to Maria, this work would have never happened. Thank you for igniting my healing journey and being the most love-filled soul sister. I'm so grateful to walk through Earth School alongside you.

Stacey, Stacey, Stacey. Your ebullience and enthusiasm are unmatched. Thank you for being such a beautiful friend and champion of my work—without you this would have remained a draft on my computer. You have touched my life in immeasurable ways, and I love you to life.

Maria Shriver, it is a profound honor to be part of your imprint. Thank you for your devotion to uplifting and enriching women around the world. You are a shining example of what it means to use influence in service of healing and meaningful change. Thank you for sharing your platform and amplifying underrecognized voices like mine. The world needs more visionary leaders like you.

Mama, thank you for birthing me. I remember when I first went to life-coaching and made a long list of everything I needed to take accountability for. You listened with the most love and least judgment, and to me, that sums up who you are: an ever-loving, free spirit who just wants to put a chandelier in every room. Thank you for reminding me to take mental health days, to make everything libra-beautiful, and to have a lot more fun along the way.

Dad. It's been complicated, and I love you with all my heart. I always wanted to get to know you more, because it felt like meeting more of myself. Thank you for your complexity; it's helped me further honor my own. You are undeniably brilliant and have lived through some shit. This work wouldn't be possible if I hadn't witnessed both your struggles and your triumphs. Thank you for choosing this twisty lifetime.

Granny. Little, tiny granny. You came from poverty and built the most beautiful life for us all. I'm crying as I type this. There would be no book if it weren't for you. Thank you for saying yes to your dreams so we could all say yes to ours. Thank you for being an ever-inspiring entrepreneur before women could have loans and credit cards. Thank you for showing me what creating a mini-economy and lifting a whole community looks like. Thank you for showing me what leading a business with your intuition looks like. I know you were deeply misunderstood, but thank you for choosing to keep going especially when others didn't get it. And thank you for sharing your love of jewels with me. Whenever I hear the jingle of an armload of bangles, I know you are beside me.

Gramps, up in heaven. You were my first experience of unconditional love. Everyone needs and deserves that. I miss you every single day and I wish you would visit me more. Some days, as I was writing, I could feel your calloused hand in mine. I'd also hear the former headmaster in you say that you'd give me demerits for typing this instead of writing it out. Please watch over this work and let it become what it needs to be. Thank you for being my guardian angel . . . feel free to send more help!

Jidu, whom I only knew on this earthly plane for a short while. Thank you for being my spiritual custodian and holding me in integrity. Whenever the universe gives me a fierce little nudge, I know it's you.

To my beloved sisters, I am because you are. What a special thing it has been to be born into this group of fierce, brilliant, justice-oriented women. There has been no greater joy nor privilege.

Last, but most certainly not least, I want to thank myself. To the younger me, who had the courage to seek therapy at twenty-one and begin the process of healing, thank you for choosing transformation. To the version of me who was unwell, who had the strength to forge a new path when the old one was crumbling, thank you for your wisdom. To the discouraged me, who kept moving forward—sometimes working every single day to make this dream a reality—thank you for your perseverance. And to the ambitious me who authored this book and dared to rewrite a majorly broken script—thank you for your audacity. I hope this book serves as a reminder that no dream is too big, especially when you have an amazing group of humans around you.

NOTES

Epigraph

1. *Rilke's Book of Hours: Love Poems to God*, trans. Anita Barrows and Joanne Macy (Riverhead Books, 1996).

Author's Note

1. Mia L. Carey, PhD, and Amber A. Hewitt, PhD, "Words Matter: A Guide to Inclusive Language Around Racial and Ethnic Diversity," Office of Human Rights, Government of the District of Columbia, April 2023, ohr.dc.gov/sites/default/files/dc/sites/ohr/page_content/attachments /OHR_ORE_RacialEquity_ILG_April2023.pdf.
2. Carey and Hewitt, "Words Matter."
3. NEA Center for Social Justice, "Toolkit: White Supremacy Culture Resources," NEA: National Education Association, December 2020, nea.org/resource-library/white-supremacy-culture-resources.

Introduction

1. Liz Elting, "The High Cost of Ambition: Why Women Are Held Back for Thinking Big," *Forbes*, April 24, 2017, forbes.com/sites/lizelting /2017/04/24/the-high-cost-of-ambition-why-women-are-held-back-for -thinking-big.

2. "Serena Williams Tells Chair Umpire: 'I Don't Cheat to Win, I'd Rather Lose,'" CBS News, September 8, 2018, cbsnews.com/news/serena-williams-us-open-penalties-naomi-osaka-today-live-updates-2018-09-08.

3. "US Open 2018: Serena Williams Accuses Umpire of Sexism After Outbursts in Final," BBC, September 9, 2018, bbc.com/sport/tennis/45461716.

4. Siri Chilazi, "Advancing Gender Equality in Venture Capital," Women and Public Policy Program, Harvard Kennedy School, October 2019, hks.harvard.edu/centers/wappp/research/past/venture-capital-entrepreneurship.

5. Kara K. Nesvig, "Reformation Founder Yael Aflalo Resigns After Allegations of Racism," *Teen Vogue*, June 14, 2020, teenvogue.com/story/reformation-founder-yael-aflalo-apologizes-for-past-racist-behavior.

6. Rachel Tashjian, "What Happened to Man Repeller?," *GQ*, December 4, 2020, gq.com/story/what-happened-to-man-repeller.

7. Mary Hanbury, "Away's Co-CEO Steph Korey to Step Down from the Role for the Second Time in Less than a Year," *Business Insider*, July 3, 2020, businessinsider.com/aways-co-ceo-steph-korey-will-step-down-this-year-2020-7.

8. "Away Co-CEO Steps down as Silicon Valley Elite Conversation Gets Leaked," CNET, July 3, 2020, cnet.com/tech/tech-industry/away-co-ceo-steps-down-as-silicon-valley-elite-conversation-gets-leaked.

Chapter 1: Painful Ambition Versus Purposeful Ambition

1. Jim Rohn, *The Power of Ambition: Awakening the Powerful Force Within You* (Sound Wisdom, 2022), 9.

2. Lise Bourbeau, *Heal Your Wounds and Find Your True Self* (Les Editions E.T.C., 2000), 17–18.

3. Bourbeau, *Heal Your Wounds and Find Your True Self*, 135.

4. Bourbeau, *Heal Your Wounds and Find Your True Self*, 17.

5. Bourbeau, *Heal Your Wounds and Find Your True Self*, 17.

6. Aysa Gray, "The Bias of 'Professionalism' Standards," *Stanford Social Innovation Review*, June 4, 2019, ssir.org/articles/entry/the_bias_of_professionalism_standards.

7. Megan Hellerer, "NO MORE 'HUSTLE': Making the Shift from 'Blind Ambition' to 'Aligned Ambition,'" Medium, February 14, 2020, medium.com/wtf-am-i-doing-with-my-life/no-more-hustle-making -the-shift-from-blind-ambition-to-aligned-ambition-f5a5056bbe23; Rha Goddess, rhagoddess.com, accessed August 27, 2024.

Chapter 2: Mindsets That Disrupt Our Unfolding

1. Jeff Brown, *Ascending with Both Feet on the Ground* (Pipik Press, 2012), 54.
2. Carl Jung, *Aion: Researches into the Phenomenology of the Self*, trans. R. F. C. Hull (Princeton University Press, 1959), 71.
3. Tony Gaskins (@TonyGaskins), "You teach people how to treat you by what you allow, what you stop, and what you reinforce. Know that!," Twitter (now X), January 16, 2013, x.com/TonyGaskins/status /291748201919295488.
4. Rha Goddess, *The Calling: 3 Fundamental Shifts to Stay True, Get Paid, and Do Good* (St. Martin's Publishing Group, 2019).
5. Gay Hendricks, *The Big Leap: Conquer Your Hidden Fear and Take Life to the Next Level* (HarperCollins, 2009), 45.
6. Hendricks, *The Big Leap*, 48.
7. Hendricks, *The Big Leap*, 52.
8. Hendricks, *The Big Leap*, 55.
9. Jill Suttie, "How to Overcome Your Brain's Fixation on Bad Things," *Greater Good*, January 13, 2020, greatergood.berkeley.edu/article/item /how_to_overcome_your_brains_fixation_on_bad_things.
10. Jonathan Sherin, PhD, and Charles B. Nemeroff, MD, PhD, "Post-traumatic Stress Disorder: The Neurobiological Impact of Psychological Trauma," *Dialogues in Clinical Neuroscience* 13, no. 3 (September 2011): 263–78, ncbi.nlm.nih.gov/pmc/articles/PMC3182008.
11. Debbie Ford, *The Dark Side of the Light Chasers: Reclaiming Your Power, Creativity, Brilliance, and Dreams* (Riverhead Books, 2010), 1.
12. Christopher Perry, "The Shadow," Society of Analytical Psychology, August 12, 2015, thesap.org.uk/articles-on-jungian-psychology-2/about -analysis-and-therapy/the-shadow.
13. Ford, *The Dark Side of the Light Chasers*, 6.
14. Ford, *The Dark Side of the Light Chasers*, 6.

15. Melody Beattie, *Codependent No More: How to Stop Controlling Others and Start Caring for Yourself* (Spiegel & Grau, 2022), 34.
16. Terri Cole, *Too Much: A Guide to Breaking the Cycle of High-Functioning Codependency* (Sounds True, 2024), 21.
17. Brené Brown, *The Gifts of Imperfection: Let Go of Who You Think You're Supposed to Be and Embrace Who You Are* (Hazelden Publishing, 2010), 38.
18. Hendricks, *The Big Leap*, 20.

Chapter 3: The Systems and Ideologies That Keep Us Trapped

1. Anne Helen Petersen, *Can't Even: How Millennials Became the Burnout Generation* (Houghton Mifflin Harcourt, 2020), xxii.
2. Adrian Horton, "Hustle Harder: How TV Became Obsessed with Stories of Workism," *The Guardian*, March 31, 2022, theguardian.com/tv-and-radio/2022/mar/31/wecrashed-hustle-harder-tv-workism.
3. "Black and Latino Students Shut Out of Advanced Coursework Opportunities," EdTrust, January 9, 2020, edtrust.org/press-release/black-and-latino-students-shut-out-of-advanced-coursework-opportunities.
4. Isabella Rosario, "When the 'Hustle' Isn't Enough," Code Switch, April 3, 2020, npr.org/sections/codeswitch/2020/04/03/826015780/when-the-hustle-isnt-enough.
5. Jan Dawson, "Travis Kalanick Has No One but Himself to Blame for Uber's Toxic Company Culture," *Vox*, March 2, 2017, vox.com/2017/3/2/14794092/uber-ceo-travis-kalanick-company-culture-toxic-values.
6. Rosario, "When the 'Hustle' Isn't Enough."
7. Rani Molla and Shirin Ghaffary, "The WeWork Mess, Explained," *Vox*, October 22, 2019, vox.com/recode/2019/9/23/20879656/wework-mess-explained-ipo-softbank.
8. Eva Leonard, "How Neon Lights Up WeWork Space," WeWork, July 3, 2019, wework.com/ideas/workspace-solutions/flexible-products/how-neon-lights-up-wework-space.
9. "Long Working Hours Increasing Deaths from Heart Disease and Stroke: WHO, ILO," World Health Organization, May 17, 2021, who.int/news/item/17-05-2021-long-working-hours-increasing-deaths-from-heart-disease-and-stroke-who-ilo.

10. Christin L. Munsch and Lindsey T. O'Connor, "Gender and the Disparate Payoffs of Overwork," *Social Psychology Quarterly* 87, no. 1 (January 11, 2023), doi.org/10.1177/01902725221141059.

11. Kristy Threlkeld, "Employee Burnout Report: COVID-19's Impact and 3 Strategies to Curb It," Indeed, updated July 11, 2024, indeed.com/lead /preventing-employee-burnout-report.

12. "The Squeezed Middle: Millennial Managers Worse Off while Supporting a Burnt-Out Workforce," MetLife, September 17, 2021, metlife.com /about-us/newsroom/2021/september/the-squeezed-middle--millennial -managers-worse-off-while-supporting-a-burnt-out-workforce.

13. Sean Illing, "How Millennials Became the Burnout Generation," *Vox*, December 3, 2020, vox.com/policy-and-politics/21473579/millennials-great -recession-burnout-anne-helen-petersen.

14. Lamya Khoury, Yilang L. Tang, Bekh Bradley, Joe F. Cubells, and Kerry J. Ressler, "Substance Use, Childhood Traumatic Experience, and Post-traumatic Stress Disorder in an Urban Civilian Population," *Depression and Anxiety* (November 3, 2010): 1077–86, doi.org/10.1002/da.20751.

15. Donna Portland, *Positive Habits Get Results* (Balboa Press, 2020).

16. Shannon McLellan, "This Doctor Helps Olympians with Their Sleep. Here Are His Tips to Sleep like a Champion," *Good Morning America*, July 26, 2021, goodmorningamerica.com/wellness/story/doctor -helps-olympians-sleep-tips-sleep-champion-78864523.

17. "Gender Equality Is Stalling: 131 Years to Close the Gap," WeForum, June 20, 2023, weforum.org/press/2023/06/gender-equality-is-stalling -131-years-to-close-the-gap.

18. "Global Gender Gap Report 2022," World Economic Forum, July 13, 2022, weforum.org/publications/global-gender-gap-report-2022.

19. "The Wage Gap Among LGBTQ+ Workers in the United States," Human Rights Campaign, November 17, 2021, hrc.org/resources/the-wage -gap-among-lgbtq-workers-in-the-united-states.

20. Elise Gould, "Gender Wage Gap Persists in 2023," Economic Policy Institute, March 8, 2024, epi.org/blog/gender-wage-gap-persists-in-2023 -women-are-paid-roughly-22-less-than-men-on-average; Sarah Javaid, "Native Women Lose More Than $1.1 Million to the Racist and Sexist Wage Gap over a 40-Year Career," National Women's Law Center, November 2023, nwlc.org/wp-content/uploads/2022/11/NWEPD-2023.pdf.

21. Alexandra Cawthorne Gaines, "The Straight Facts on Women in Poverty," Center for American Progress, October 8, 2008, americanprogress .org/article/the-straight-facts-on-women-in-poverty.

22. Pauline Rose Clance and Suzanne Ament Imes, "The Imposter Phenomenon in High Achieving Women: Dynamics and Therapeutic Intervention,"

Psychotherapy: Theory, Research & Practice 15, no. 3 (1978): 241–47, doi.org/10.1037/h0086006.

23. Kess Eruteya, "You're Not an Imposter. You're Actually Pretty Amazing," *Harvard Business Review*, January 3, 2022, hbr.org/2022/01/youre-not-an-imposter-youre-actually-pretty-amazing.

24. Ruchika Tulshyan and Jodi-Ann Burey, "Stop Telling Women They Have Imposter Syndrome," *Harvard Business Review*, February 11, 2021, hbr.org/2021/02/stop-telling-women-they-have-imposter-syndrome.

25. Tyece Wilkins, "A Point of View: The Privilege of Second Chances," Inclusion Solution, March 1, 2018, theinclusionsolution.me/point-view-privilege-second-chances.

26. Amy Edmonson, "Psychological Safety," Amy C. Edmondson, amycedmondson.com/psychological-safety.

27. Anagha Srikanth, "New Study Finds White Male Minority Rule Dominates US," Changing America, *The Hill*, May 26, 2021, thehill.com/changing-america/respect/diversity-inclusion/555503-new-study-finds-white-male-minority-rule.

28. Deepa Purushothaman, *The First, the Few, the Only: How Women of Color Can Redefine Power in Corporate America* (HarperCollins, 2022), 18.

29. "Women in the Workplace 2022," McKinsey & Company, October 18, 2022, mckinsey.com/~/media/mckinsey/featured%20insights/diversity%20and%20inclusion/women%20in%20the%20workplace%202022/women-in-the-workplace-2022.pdf.

30. "Women in the Workplace 2021," Lean In, September 2021, leanin.org/women-in-the-workplace/2021/women-of-color-continue-to-have-a-worse-experience-at-work.

31. Michelle K. Ryan and S. Alexander Haslam, "The Glass Cliff: Exploring the Dynamics Surrounding the Appointment of Women to Precarious Leadership Positions," *Academy of Management Review* 32, no. 2 (April 2007): 549–72, jstor.org/stable/20159315.

32. Michelle K. Ryan and S. Alexander Haslam, "The Glass Cliff: Evidence That Women Are Over-Represented in Precarious Leadership Positions," *British Journal of Management* 16 (February 9, 2005), doi.org/10.1111/j.1467-8551.2005.00433.x.

33. Kristen Munson, "Studies Show Women & Minority Leaders Have Shorter Tenures, Tenuous Support," Utah State University, July 18, 2013, usu.edu/today/story/studies-show-women-amp-minority-leaders-have-shorter-tenures-tenuous-support.

34. Alison Cook and Christy Glass, "Glass Cliffs and Organizational Saviors: Barriers to Minority Leadership in Work Organizations?," *Social Problems* 60, no. 2 (May 1, 2013), doi.org/10.1525/sp.2013.60.2.168.

35. Zuhairah Washington and Laura Morgan Roberts, "Women of Color Get Less Support at Work. Here's How Managers Can Change That," *Harvard Business Review*, March 4, 2019, hbr.org/2019/03/women-of-color-get-less-support-at-work-heres-how-managers-can-change-that.

36. "Being Black in Corporate America: An Intersectional Exploration," Center for Talent Innovation, 2019, talentinnovation.org/_private/assets/BeingBlack-KeyFindings-CTI.pdf.

37. "The Similar-to-Me Effect," The Decision Lab, thedecisionlab.com/reference-guide/psychology/the-similar-to-me-effect.

38. "Being Black in Corporate America."

39. "Women in the Workplace 2022," Lean In, 2022, leanin.org/women-in-the-workplace/2022/why-women-leaders-are-switching-jobs.

Chapter 4: Honor Your Purpose

1. Marianne Williamson, *A Return to Love: Reflections on the Principles of* A Course in Miracles (HarperPerennial, 1992), 179.

2. Helaine Selin, ed., *Nature Across Cultures: Views of Nature and the Environment in Non-Western Cultures (Science Across Cultures: The History of Non-Western Science, 4)* (Springer, 2003), 329.

3. Stephen Cope, *The Great Work of Your Life: A Guide for the Journey to Your True Calling* (Bantam Books, 2012), xviii.

4. "Endocrine Disruptors," National Institute of Environmental Health Sciences, accessed September 26, 2024, niehs.nih.gov/health/topics/agents/endocrine.

5. Radoslaw Balwierz et al., "Potential Carcinogens in Makeup Cosmetics," *International Journal of Environmental Research and Public Health* 20, no. 6 (March 8, 2023): 4780, doi.org/10.3390/ijerph20064780.

6. "Workplace Burnout Survey: Burnout Without Borders," Deloitte, 2015, deloitte.com/us/en/pages/about-deloitte/articles/burnout-survey.html.

7. Erin A Cech, "Striking a Balance Between Your Passion and Your Paycheck," *Harvard Business Review*, October 13, 2022, hbr.org/2022/10/striking-a-balance-between-your-passion-and-your-paycheck.

8. Amina AlTai, host, *Amina Change Your Life*, season 1, episode 74, "The Power of Applied Empathy with Michael Ventura," June 18, 2024, 23 min., 32 sec., podcasts.apple.com/us/podcast/ep-74-the-power

-of-applied-empathy-with-michael-ventura/id1669584137?i=10006593
73519.

9. "Striving for Balance, Advocating for Change: The Deloitte Global 2022 Gen Z & Millennial Survey," Deloitte, 2022, deloitte.com/content/dam /assets-shared/legacy/docs/about/2022/deloitte-2022-genz-millennial -survey.pdf.

10. "How Generation Z Will Impact the Future of Work," Cigna Group, accessed September 26, 2024, newsroom.cigna.com/how-generation-z-will -impact-the-future-of-work.

11. "A Call for Accountability and Action: The Deloitte Global 2021 Gen Z & Millennial Survey," Deloitte, 2021, deloitte.com/content/dam/assets -shared/legacy/docs/insights/2022/2021-deloitte-global-millennial -survey-report.pdf.

12. Irregular Labs, "The Irregular Report: Gender, Activism, and Gen Z," Irregular Report, April 10, 2019, medium.com/irregular-labs/the-irregular -report-gender-activism-and-gen-z-f8728212ef19.

13. Doris Lam, "Gen Z Prioritises Period Self-Care More Than Millennials, New Study Finds," *Tatler Asia*, April 11, 2022, tatlerasia.com/lifestyle /wellbeing/period-self-care-new-study; Shelby Smith, "Setting Boundaries: Why Quiet Quitting Is a Form of Self-Care for Generation-Z," Girls United, *Essence*, updated May 1, 2024, girlsunited.essence.com/article /quiet-quitting-gen-z-self-care.

Chapter 5: Identify Your True Gifts

1. Stephen Cope, "The Gift: Living a Life of Purpose and Meaning," Stephen Cope, September 30, 2012, stephencope.com/articles-by-stephen /the-gift-living-a-life-of-purpose-and-meaning.

2. Emma Heaps, "Comfort, Stretch and Don't Panic!," Training Industry, November 13, 2017, trainingindustry.com/articles/performance -management/comfort-stretch-and-dont-panic.

3. Cope, "The Gift."

4. Kristi Walker, Kristen Bialik, and Patrick Van Kessel, "Strong Men, Caring Women: How Americans Describe What Society Values (and Doesn't) in Each Gender," Pew Research Center, July 24, 2018, pewre search.org/social-trends/interactives/strong-men-caring-women.

5. Jess Staufenberg, "Black and Female Professors Not Seen as 'Geniuses' as Often as White Male Professors," *The Independent*, March

4, 2016, independent.co.uk/news/science/black-and-female-professors
-not-seen-as-geniuses-as-often-as-white-men-by-students-a6911121
.html.

6. Herbert Muschamp, "An Iraqi-Born Woman Wins Pritzker Architecture Award," *New York Times*, March 22, 2004, nytimes.com/2004
/03/22/arts/an-iraqi-born-woman-wins-pritzker-architecture-award
.html.

7. Tasminda K. Dhaliwal et al., "Educator Bias Is Associated with Racial Disparities in Student Achievement and Discipline," Brookings Institution, July 20, 2020, brookings.edu/articles/educator-bias-is-associated
-with-racial-disparities-in-student-achievement-and-discipline.

8. Angela Lee Duckworth, Patrick D. Quinn, Ronald R. Lynam, Rolf Loeber, and Magda Stouthamer-Loeber, "Role of Test Motivation in Intelligence Testing," *Psychological and Cognitive Sciences* 108, no. 19 (2011), doi.org/10.1073/pnas.1018601108.

9. Jessica Leber, "Americans Think Geniuses Are Men: Inside Our Contradictory Attitudes on Brilliance," *Fast Company*, February 25, 2015, fastcompany.com/3042773/americans-think-geniuses-are-men-inside
-our-contradictory-attitudes-on-brilliance.

10. Lin Bian, Sarah-Jane Leslie, and Andrei Cimpian, "Gender Stereotypes About Intellectual Ability Emerge Early and Influence Children's Interests," *Science*, January 27, 2017, doi.org/DOI: 10.1126/science
.aah6524.

11. Christine Battersby, *Gender and Genius: Towards a Feminist Aesthetics* (Indiana University Press, 1990), 14.

12. Holly Honderich, Natalie Sherman, and Erin Delmore, "Everyone Got Duped by Sam Bankman-Fried's Big Gamble," BBC, March 28, 2024, bbc.com/news/world-us-canada-67302950.

13. Britney Nguyen, "Sam Bankman-Fried Was Once Caught Playing the Video Game 'League of Legends' During a Pitch Meeting for FTX," *Business Insider*, November 10, 2022, businessinsider.com/ftx-sam-bankman
-fried-league-of-legends-investor-pitch-meeting-2022-11.

14. Brittany Packnett Cunningham, "How to Build Your Confidence—and Spark It in Others," TED Talk, April 2019, video, 13 min., 20 sec., ted
.com/talks/brittany_packnett_cunningham_how_to_build_your_con
fidence_and_spark_it_in_others.

Chapter 6: Meet Your Needs

1. Kate Northrup, "It's OK to Have a Need," December 16, 2018, You-Tube, 6:05, youtube.com/watch?v=QIh39sINR-Q.

2. Stephanie Stephens, "The CDC and AMA Agree: Racism Is a Serious Public Health Threat," AAD Career Compass, April 22, 2021, health ecareers.com/aad/career-resources/industry-news/the-cdc-and-ama -agree-racism-is-a-serious-public-health-threat.

3. Ruth-Alma N. Turkson-Ocran et al., "Discrimination Is Associated with Elevated Cardiovascular Disease Risk Among African Immigrants in the African Immigrant Health Study," *Ethnicity & Disease* 30, no. 4 (Autumn 2020): 651–60, ncbi.nlm.nih.gov/pmc/articles /PMC7518540.

4. "Individualism: I'm the Only One," White Supremacy Culture, last updated August 2023, whitesupremacyculture.info/individualism .html.

5. Emily A. Shrider, Melissa Kollar, Frances Chen, and Jessica Semega, "Income and Poverty in the United States: 2020," United States Census Bureau, September 14, 2021, census.gov/content/dam/Census/library /publications/2021/demo/p60-273.pdf.

6. Lindsay Tigar, "4 Women on How They Reached a Six-Figure Salary," HerMoney, March 25, 2021, hermoney.com/earn/salaries /4-women-on-how-they-reached-a-six-figure-salary.

7. Eilene Zimmerman, "Only 2% of Women-Owned Businesses Break the $1 Million Mark—Here's How to Be One of Them," *Forbes*, April 1, 2015, forbes.com/sites/eilenezimmerman/2015/04/01/only-2-of-women -owned-businesses-break-the-1-million-mark-heres-how-to-be-one -of-them/?sh=5d657bf427a6.

8. Ashley Bittner and Brigette Lau, "Women-Led Startups Received Just 2.3% of VC Funding in 2020," *Harvard Business Review*, February 25, 2021, hbr.org/2021/02/women-led-startups-received-just-2-3 -of-vc-funding-in-2020.

9. HRC Foundation, "The Wage Gap Among LGBTQ+ Workers in the United States," Human Rights Campaign, accessed September 26, 2024, hrc.org/resources/the-wage-gap-among-lgbtq-workers-in-the-united -states.

10. Marc Folch, "The LGBTQ+ Gap: Recent Estimates for Young Adults in the United States," April 7, 2022, dx.doi.org/10.2139/ssrn.4072893.

11. Charlotte J. Patterson, Martin-José Sepúlveda, and Jordyn White, eds., *Understanding the Well-Being of LGBTQI+ Populations* (National Academies Press, 2020).

12. "Annual Median Earnings for People with and Without Disabilities in the U.S. from 2008 to 2021," Statista, accessed January 16, 2023, statista.com/statistics/978989/disability-annual-earnings-us.

13. John Elflein, "Poverty Rate Among People with and Without Disabilities in the U.S. from 2008 to 2022," Statista, May 6, 2024, statista.com/statistics/979003/disability-poverty-rate-us.

14. "Poverty Rate by Race/Ethnicity," KFF, June 3, 2021, kff.org/other/state-indicator/poverty-rate-by-raceethnicity/?currentTimeframe=0&sortModel=%7B%22colId%22:%22Location%22,%22sort%22:%22asc%22%7D.

15. Emily Moss et al., "The Black-White Wealth Gap Left Black Households More Vulnerable," Brookings Institution, December 8, 2020, brookings.edu/blog/up-front/2020/12/08/the-black-white-wealth-gap-left-black-households-more-vulnerable.

16. Maggie Germano, "How Women Can Change the World with Their Money Choices," *Forbes*, updated December 15, 2020, forbes.com/sites/maggiegermano/2020/09/22/how-women-can-change-the-world-with-their-money-choices.

17. Amina AlTai, host, *Amina Change Your Life*, season 1, episode 13, "Economic Justice and Building an Economically Just Business Model with Kelly Diels," April 11, 2023, 40 min., podcasts.apple.com/au/podcast/ep-13-economic-justice-and-building-an-economically/id1669584137?i=1000608474481.

Chapter 7: Prioritize Contentment

1. Daniel Cordaro, PhD, "What If You Pursued Contentment Rather Than Happiness?," University of Chicago, May 27, 2020, wisdomcenter.uchicago.edu/news/wisdom-news/what-if-you-pursued-contentment-rather-happiness.

2. Robert Lustig, *The Hacking of the American Mind: The Science Behind the Corporate Takeover of Our Bodies and Brains* (Avery, 2008), 8.

3. Ethan S. Bromberg-Martin, Masayuki Matsumoto, and Okihide Hikosaka, "Dopamine in Motivational Control: Rewarding, Aversive, and

Alerting," *Neuron* 68, no. 5 (December 9, 2010): 815–34, doi:10.1016 /j.neuron.2010.11.022.

4. Penny Locaso, "What You Were Taught About 'Happiness' Isn't True," *Harvard Business Review*, January 12, 2021, hbr.org/2021/01/what-you -were-taught-about-happiness-isnt-true.

5. Locaso, "What You Were Taught About 'Happiness' Isn't True."

6. Jordi Quoidbach et al., "Emodiversity and the Emotional Ecosystem," *Journal of Experimental Psychology: General* 143, no. 6 (December 2014): 2057–66, doi:10.1037/a0038025.

7. Cordaro, "What If You Pursued Contentment Rather Than Happiness?"

8. Cordaro, "What If You Pursued Contentment Rather Than Happiness?"

9. Paul Ingram and Yoonjin Choi, "What Does Your Company Really Stand For?," *Harvard Business Review Magazine*, November–December 2022, hbr.org/2022/11/what-does-your-company-really-stand-for.

10. Brian A. Primack et al., "Use of Multiple Social Media Platforms and Symptoms of Depression and Anxiety: A Nationally-Representative Study Among U.S. Young Adults," *Computers in Human Behavior* 69 (April 2017): 1–9, doi.org/10.1016/j.chb.2016.11.013.

11. Judith B. White et al., "Frequent Social Comparisons and Destructive Emotions and Behaviors: The Dark Side of Social Comparisons," *Journal of Adult Development* 13, no. 1 (June 14, 2006): 36–44, doi.org/DOI: 10.1007/s10804-006-9005-0.

12. Julianne Holt-Lunstad, Timothy B. Smith, and J. Bradley Layton, "Social Relationships and Mortality Risk: A Meta-analytic Review," *PLOS Medicine* (July 27, 2010): 113–22, doi.org/10.1371/journal.pmed .1000316.

13. Deepa Purushothamana, *The First, the Few, the Only: How Women of Color Can Redefine Power in Corporate America* (HarperCollins, 2022), 127.

14. Kate Johnson, "Radical Friendship: A Conversation Between Tara Brach and Kate Johnson," interview by Tara Brach, Kate Johnson, video, 1:08:51, katejohnson.com/journal/radical-friendship-a-conversation-between-tara -brach-and-kate-johnson.

15. Marc Schulz and Robert Waldinger, "An 85-Year Harvard Study Found the No. 1 Thing That Makes Us Happy in Life: It Helps Us 'Live Longer,'" CNBC, updated February 10, 2023, cnbc.com/2023/02/10/85

-year-harvard-study-found-the-secret-to-a-long-happy-and-successful
-life.html.

16. Purushothamana, *The First, the Few, the Only*, 127.

17. Cale D. Magnuson and Lynn A. Barnett, "The Playful Advantage: How Playfulness Enhances Coping with Stress," *Leisure Sciences* 35, no. 2 (March 20, 2013): 129–44, doi.org/10.1080/01490400.2013.761905; René T. Prover, "The Well-being of Playful Adults: Adult Playfulness, Subjective Well-Being, Physical Well-Being, and the Pursuit of Enjoyable Activities," *European Journal of Humour Research* 1, no. 1 (March 2013): 84–98, doi.org/10.7592/EJHR2013.1.1.proyer.

18. Krystyna S. Aune and Norman C. Wong, "Antecedents and Consequences of Adult Play in Romantic Relationships," *Personal Relationships* 9, no. 3 (December 17, 2002): 279–86, doi.org/10.1111/1475-6811.00019.

19. Samuel West, "Playing at Work: Organizational Play as a Facilitator of Creativity" (PhD diss., Lund University, 2015).

20. René T. Prover, "A New Structural Model for the Study of Adult Playfulness: Assessment and Exploration of an Understudied Individual Differences Variable," *Personality and Individual Difference* 108 (April 1, 2017): 113–22, doi.org/10.1016/j.paid.2016.12.011.

Chapter 8: Take Aligned Action

1. *The Marvelous Mrs. Maisel*, season 5, episode 9, "Four Minutes," written and directed by Amy Sherman-Palladino, aired May 26, 2023, on Amazon Prime Video.

2. George T. Doran, "There's a S.M.A.R.T. Way to Management Goals and Objectives," Temple University, November 1, 1981, https://community .mis.temple.edu/mis0855002fall2015/files/2015/10/S.M.A.R.T-Way -Management-Review.pdf; "Are SMART Goals Dumb?," Leadership IQ, accessed August 13, 2024, leadershipiq.com/blogs/leadershipiq/35353793 -are-smart-goals-dumb.

3. "Kind," Online Etymology Dictionary, accessed September 26, 2024, etymonline.com/word/kind.

4. *Unbreakable Kimmy Schmidt*, season 1, episode 2, "Kimmy Gets a Job!," written by Tina Fey, Robert Carlock, and Sam Means, directed by Tristram Shapeero, aired March 5, 2015, on Netflix.

5. *Indiana Jones and the Last Crusade*, directed by Stephen Spielberg (1989; Paramount Pictures).

6. Ethan Kross et al., "Social Rejection Shares Somatosensory Representations with Physical Pain," *Proceedings of the National Academy of Sciences of the United States of America*, 108, no. 15 (March 28, 2011): 6270–75, doi.org/10.1073/pnas.1102693108.

7. Brené Brown, "Dr. Brené Brown: You Might Be Afraid and Not Even Know It," *SuperSoul Sunday*, posted March 15, 2013, by OWN, YouTube, 2:22, youtube.com/watch?v=WsbdKN--m5I.

8. "Childhood Trauma Leads to Brains Wired for Fear," Side Effects Public Media, February 3, 2015, sideeffectspublicmedia.org/community-health/2015-02-03/childhood-trauma-leads-to-brains-wired-for-fear.

9. Farzana Saleem, Riana E. Anderson, and Monnica Williams, "Addressing the 'Myth' of Racial Trauma: Developmental and Ecological Considerations for Youth of Color," *Clinical Child and Family Psychology Review* 23 (October 23, 2019): 1–14, doi.org/10.1007/s10567-019-00304-1; Jake Lowary, "Study Finds LGBQ People Report Higher Rates of Adverse Childhood Experiences than Straight People, Worse Mental Health as Adults," Vanderbilt University Medical Center, February 24, 2022, news.vumc.org/2022/02/24/study-finds-lgbq-people-report-higher-rates-of-adverse-childhood-experiences-than-straight-people-worse-mental-health-as-adults; Miranda Olff, PhD, and Willemien Langeland, PhD, "Why Men and Women May Respond Differently to Psychological Trauma," *Psychiatric Times* 39, no. 4 (April 27, 2022), psychiatrictimes.com/view/why-men-and-women-may-respond-differently-to-psychological-trauma; Margaret Charlton, PhD, et al., "Facts on Traumatic Stress and Children with Developmental Disabilities," National Child Traumatic Stress Network, 2004, nctsn.org/sites/default/files/resources//traumatic_stress_and_children_with_developmental_disabilities.pdf.

10. Bessel van der Kolk, MD, *The Body Keeps the Score* (Penguin Books, 2014), 208.

11. Thekla Morgenroth, Michelle K. Ryan, and Cordelia Fine, "The Gendered Consequences of Risk-Taking at Work: Are Women Averse to Risk or to Poor Consequences?," *Psychology of Women Quarterly* 46, no. 3 (April 18, 2022), doi.org/10.1177/03616843221084048.

12. Margery Williams, *The Velveteen Rabbit* (Doubleday Books for Young Readers, 1922), penguinrandomhouse.ca/books/191202/the-velveteen -rabbit-by-margery-williams-illustrated-by-william-nicholson/978038 5375665/excerpt.

Conclusion

1. Online Etymology Dictionary, "devotion (n.)," etymonline.com/word /devotion#etymonline_v_8492.

INDEX